The Battle Of Wilson's Creek

by

Edwin C. Bearss

with battle maps by David Whitman

published by

George Washington Carver

Birthplace District Association

1975

ARTCRAFT PRINTERS UNION LABEL BOZEMAN, MONTANA

i

SMOKE

I sit in a chair and read the newspapers.

Millions of men go to war, acres af them are
buried, guns and ships broken, cities
burned, villages sent up in smoke,
and children where cows are killed off
amid hoarse barbecues vanish like
finger-rings of smoke in a north wind.

I sit in a chair and read the newspapers.

—CARL SANDBURG.

Contents

After Governor Jackson and his forces lost the Battle of Boonville, they retreated south. Their route of retreat took them from Boonville through Warsaw, Montevallo, Lamar, Carthage, and finally to Cowskin Prairie in the extreme southwest corner of Missouri. As General Lyon and his forces pursued Governor Jackson's army, they passed through Georgetown, Clinton, Osceola, and Stockton to reach their destination — Springfield.

About the Author

Edwin C. Bearss was born in Billings, Mont., on June 26, 1923. He grew up on a ranch near Hardin, Mont., in the shadow of the Rosebud Mountains within a bicycle ride of Custer Battlefield. On the ranch, the E Bar S, he named the cattle for Civil War generals and battles.

He attended a one-room school until he went to St. John's Military Academy in Delafield, Wis., in 1937. He graduated from Hardin High School and joined the Marine Corps. During World War II he was with the 3rd Marine Raider Battalion and 1st Marine Division in the invasions of Guadacanal and New Britain. He was wounded and spent 26 months in various hospitals.

Mr. Bearss studied at Georgetown University receiving a degree in Foreign Service. He worked for 3 years at the Navy Hydrographic Office in Suitland, Md.

Later, at Indiana University, he received his M.A. degree in history. His National Park Service career began in 1955 at Vicksburg, Miss., where he was park historian. While he was at Vicksburg, he did the research leading him and two friends to the long-lost resting place of the Union gunboat CAIRO. He located the two long overlooked forts at Grand Gulf, Miss., and helped get Grand Gulf made into a State park. He was the founder of the Mississippi Civil War Round Table which later consolidated with the Jackson Civil War Round Table, a newer group.

Mr. Bearss was chosen Man of the Year at Vicksburg in 1963. He received the Harry Truman Award for Meritorius Service in the field of Civil War history. More than a hundred of his historical articles have appeared in scholarly journals.

He is married to the former Margie Riddle of Brandon, Miss., and they have three children — Sara, born in 1960; Edwin Cole, Jr., born in 1962; and Virginia, born in 1965.

He has done detailed studies for the National Park Service in many areas — Vicksburg, Pea Ridge, Wilson's Creek, the Ray House, Fort Smith, Stones River, Fort Donelson, battles around Richmond, Bighorn Canyon, Eisenhower Farm, the gold miners' route over Chilkoot Pass, Alaska, the Lyndon B. Johnson Ranch, Fort Moultrie, Fort Point, William Howard Taft House, Fort Hancock, and Herbert Hoover National Historic Site.

Previous Books by the Author

Books written:

Decision in Mississippi

Steele's Retreat from Camden

Rebel Victory at Vicksburg

Hardluck Ironclad: Sinking and Salvage of the "Cairo"

Fort Smith: Little Gibraltor on the Arkansas (in collaboration with A. M. Gibson)

Books edited:

A Southern Record: The Story of the 3rd Louisiana Infantry

A Louisiana Confederate: Felix Pierre Poche

Memoirs of a Confederate: Historic and Personal

Introduction

As early as 1818, Missouri, then a territory, was deeply involved in the struggle which erupted into civil war. The slavery question had not been injected into national politics until Missouri petitioned for its statehood. A great national debate followed over the extension of slavery. This debate continued until the last shot was fired in 1865.

Missourians moved from debate to open warfare when they tried to force slavery on free soil Kansas settlers in 1854. There followed 3 years of murder, looting, and burning by both sides. Missourians gave up their efforts in the "Bloody Kansas" affair when faced with overwhelming odds. Consequently, Missourians turned from regional conflicts to the ominous national conflict which was building yearly.

What was the situation for Missourians as the new year 1860 approached? Perry McCandless, in his book *A History of Missouri, Volume II, 1820 to 1860*, summarizes it for us as follows: "Thus as the decade closed, Missouri was torn internally by the same issues that hardened the nation's sectional alignments and ultimately provoked the war between the states. This dramatic switch from the unity that had prevailed in 1820, when Missourians had united in their demands for statehood without restriction on slavery, revealed the intensification of the slavery problem and the changing nature of Missouri society that had occurred in the ensuing four decades.

" . . . The political parties that had come to represent significant values to most Missourians by 1840, and that had served as important instruments in shaping compromise and public policy, broke down in the decade of 1850's. Amid the high emotionalism a growing number of extremists on both sides of the slavery and Union questions challenged and threatened to overwhelm those who favored a course of moderation.

" . . . Missouri could properly and proudly claim a rich and diverse culture and a well-developed and varied economy, but such diversity, unfortunately, made unanimity on the problems of the day probably more difficult for Missourians to achieve than for the people of any other state in the Union. As the nation stood on the brink of disunion, Missourians faced not only their internal problems, but also the still larger question of the state's future alignment, should a division of the Union actually occur."

In 1861, Missourians could be divided into three political categories. Most desired neutrality and were called conditional Unionists. They held the North solely responsible for the deplorable condition of the country. They felt the only way to prevent dissolution of the Union was for the North to give to the South constitutional guarantees against the threatened aggressions of the abolitionists. Missourians insisted that if the North should refuse to give these guarantees and the Southern States should attempt to withdraw from the Union, the Federal Government should not undertake to coerce them to remain, but should let them go in peace.

Missourians not aligned with the majority called themselves either secessionists or unconditional Unionists. The secessionists were led by the newly elected governor, Claiborne Fox Jackson. Jackson used his position as governor to arm and enlarge the Missouri State Guard to forcefully remove Missouri from the Union.

Opposing Jackson were the unconditional Unionists led by Republican Congressman Frank Blair and U. S. Army Capt. Nathaniel Lyon. Blair used his political pull to wrangle Lyon a promotion to the rank of general and commander of the Department of the West. This placed all of the Federal military power within Missouri at Lyon's disposal.

Governor Jackson, fearful of General Lyon's new power and the impetuousness with which he might use it, requested a meeting with Lyon to formulate a compromise. After 5 hours of discussion and with no workable compromise in sight, General Lyon declared war against all secessionists within Missouri. This fateful event occurred on June 11, 1861.

Two days later, General Lyon mobilized his army and began a 2-month military campaign to drive the armed secessionists out of Missouri. Advancing up the Missouri River by steamboat, Lyon clashed with Governor Jackson's troops at Boonville on June 17 and drove them from the town. Union Col. Franz Sigel, hoping to block Jackson's retreat, engaged his troops at Carthage, Mo., July 5.

Sigel was defeated and retreated to Springfield. Having swept Sigel from his path, Jackson and his men continued southward and rendezvoused with Gen. Ben McCulloch's troops in southwest Missouri. The combined Southern forces encamped on Cowskin Prairie in the extreme southwest corner of the State. Here Gen. Sterling Price took command of the Missouri State Guard and armed and trained his green troops. General Lyon arrived in Springfield in mid-July. At this point Mr. Bearss begins his book.

David L. Whitman
Historian, George Washington Carver
National Monument

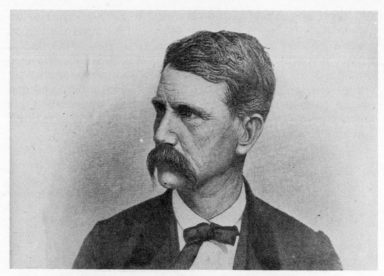

Republican Congressman Francis Blair, Jr.

Blair aided General Lyon in acquiring his promotion and in planning his campaign. He commanded a regiment at Boonville, but returned to Washington, D.C., before the Battle of Wilson's Creek.

Gov. Claiborne Fox Jackson

Governor Jackson commanded the Missouri State Guard at Boonville and Carthage until Gen. Sterling Price took command in July.

The St. Louis Arsenal in 1861

Capt. Nathaniel Lyon was transferred from Fort Riley, Kans., to the
St. Louis Arsenal where he took command on February 16, 1861.

The Battle of Boonville or
The Great Missouri "Lyon" Hunt

The Battle of Boonville was significant enough for one cartoonist to use his satirical sketch pen and produce an amusing wartime propaganda sketch.

CAVALRYMAN OF THE UNITED STATES
REGULARS, IN 1861.

THE BATTLE OF WILSON'S CREEK*

I/Lyon Occupies Springfield

The Union column commanded by Brig. Gen. Nathaniel Lyon which entered Greene County, Mo., on July 13, 1861, was made up of weary, hungry, bedraggled soldiers. Lyon was distressed to learn that the supplies which he had requested Col. Chester Harding to forward to Springfield had not arrived. Fearful lest his men plunder the Springfield business houses, Lyon had them camp in the western section of the county at Pond Springs. With this business attended to, Lyon rode into Springfield.[1]

The inhabitants of Springfield, the great majority of whom were pro-Union, were delighted and reassured by the appearance Lyon made as he galloped into town. Lyon was mounted "on his iron-gray horse, under escort of a bodyguard of ten stalwart troopers enlisted from among the German butchers of St. Louis for that especial duty." "The fearless horsemanship and defiant bearing of these bearded warriors, mounted on powerful chargers and armed to the teeth with great revolvers and massive swords, their heroic size and ferocious aspect," added luster to Lyon's entry into the city. Here, the citizens told one another, was the grim general who had captured the State troops at Camp Jackson and had forced Gov. Claiborne F. Jackson to flee from Jefferson City. Unwilling to rest on these laurels, Lyon had proceeded to disperse the army which the governor was marshaling at Boonville, and had compelled the Confederates "to fly for safety into the uttermost corner of the State."[2]

---

* Mr. Bearss has written the National Archives to have the original documents from which the **Official Records** were compiled examined to see whether the correct designation is "Wilson's Creek" or "Wilson Creek" but, up to this time, clarifying information has not been received.

As his first order of business on entering Springfield, Lyon called upon Brig. Gen. Thomas W. Sweeny and Col. Franz Sigel. (Following the defeat at Carthage on July 5, Sigel's command had fallen back to Springfield.) After having assumed charge of all the Federal troops operating in southwest Missouri, Lyon dashed off a letter to Colonel Harding reporting his safe arrival at Springfield. Next, the general turned to a discussion of the apparent breakdown in his supply line. He informed Harding that he had about 5,000 men for whom provision would have to be made. Furthermore, Lyon continued, he had failed to find at Springfield any of the supplies which he had requested to be forwarded from the St. Louis magazines. "The failure of stores reaching here," Lyon commented, "seems likely to cause serious embarrassment, which must be aggravated by continued delay, and in proportion to the time I am forced to wait for supplies." He added, "Shoes, shirts, blouses, &c., are much wanted, and I would have you furnish them, if possible, in considerable quantities."[3]

Lyon also addressed a letter to the Adjutant General in Washington asking for heavy reinforcements. To strengthen his arguments, the general observed that his effective force would "soon be reduced by discharge of three-months' volunteers to about 4,000 men, including the Illinois regiment now on the march from Rolla." Lyon estimated the Confederates would soon have a force of not less than 30,000 men with which to confront his small command. (The Union general had greatly exaggerated the Rebel strength. At this time, the Southerners could muster about 11,000 soldiers with which to contest Lyon's advance.) Consequently, Lyon informed the Washington authorities that he "must have at once an additional force of 10,000 men, or abandon my position."[4]

Two days later (on July 15), Lyon's adjutant, Maj. John M. Schofield, addressed a lengthy memorandum to Colonel Harding. Schofield informed the colonel that Lyon had about 7,000 men. But of these, he wrote, "fully one-half are three-months' volunteers, whose term of service has nearly expired, the latest expiring on the 14th of August." Like his superior, Schofield reported that Governor Jackson was concentrating his forces in the southwestern corner of Missouri, and was "receiving large re-enforcements from Arkansas, Tennessee, Louisiana, and Texas." Schofield placed the Confederate strength as "not less than 30,000

men." Unless the Federal Government promptly sent reinforcements of men and supplies, Schofield warned, Lyon
would not only have to yield the initiative, but he would be
hardpressed to hold his position.

Reporting on the condition of the troops, Schofield
observed that the soldiers were "badly clothed, poorly fed,
and imperfectly supplied with tents." Furthermore, none of
the men had been paid. He warned that "the three-months'
volunteers have become disheartened to such an extent that
very few of them are willing to renew their enlistment." In
the face of these distressing circumstances, Schofield felt
compelled to call to "the attention of the Government the
absolute necessity of sending us fresh troops at once, with
ample supplies for them and for those now here." He echoed
Lyon's request for at least 10,000 fresh troops.[5]

One day after Schofield had dispatched his message to
Harding, an order reached Springfield signed by General-in-
Chief Winfield Scott. The commander of the United States
Army in a letter dated July 5 had issued instruction directing
that five companies (B, E, F, G, and H) of the 2d U. S.
Infantry be withdrawn from the Army of the West and sent
to Washington. General Sweeny was to accompany the
five companies.[6]

In a letter to Colonel Harding dated July 17, Lyon
commented on Scott's directive. Lyon observed that three
companies of the 2d U. S. Infantry (F, G, and H) were
currently stationed at Fort Leavenworth, Kans. If these three
units were withdrawn, it would leave that important post
without a garrison. The other two units (Companies B and
E) slated for transfer to the East were in the field serving
with the general's Army of the West. If these troops were
withdrawn from his army, Lyon warned, he could "do nothing and must retire, in the absence of other troops to
supply their places." Continuing, Lyon announced that he
was "badly enough off at the best, and must utterly fail if
. . . [his] regulars all go."

Turning to the situation in the East, Lyon pointed out,
"At Washington, troops from all the Northern, Middle, and
Eastern States are available for the support of the army
in Virginia, and more are understood to be already there
than are wanted; and it seems strange that so many troops
must go on from the West and strip us of the means of
defense." Warming to his subject, he observed that if it

3

were the administration's "intention to give up the West, let it be so; it can only be the victim of imbecility or malice."

"Scott," Lyon wrote, "will cripple us if he can." The general wanted to know if Harding could "stir up this matter" and obtain some assistance for the West. Harding was urged to see Maj. Gen. John C. Frémont the moment the general reached St. Louis. (Frémont had been placed in charge of the Western Department on July 3. Frémont, however, had lingered in the East and had not yet reached his St. Louis headquarters.) Next, Lyon turned to the problem of supplying his army. The general again announced that the want of supplies had crippled his force so that he was unable to move. In conclusion, Lyon wrote, "Everything seems to combine against me at this point. Stir up [Montgomery] Blair."

A letter was also drafted by Lyon and addressed to the Assistant Adjutant General of the United States Army, Lt. Col. Edward D. Townsend. After acknowledging the receipt of Scott's order, Lyon wrote that, in answer to the Confederate activities in southwest Missouri, he had concentrated all his available troops at Springfield. He again pointed out that more than half of his aggregate strength (between 7,000 and 8,000 men) were 3-months' volunteers. The enlistment of some of these, Lyon reported, had already expired. Others would be able to claim their "discharge within a week or two," he wrote, "and the dissolution of my forces from this necessity, already commenced, will leave me less than 4,000 men, including Companies B and E," 2d U. S. Infantry, which were under orders to proceed to the East Coast.

Lyon again announced that he was confronted by a Confederate force mustering at least 30,000 officers and men. The Rebels were, he said, constantly strengthening this formidable force and accumulating arms and livestock. Hostile demonstrations by Confederate raiding parties were becoming a frequent occurrence. Lyon warned, "The evils consequent upon the withdrawal of any portion of my force will be apparent." He reasoned that if his army pulled back, the pro-Union citizens would be left without any protection. Repressed treason would "assume alarming boldness, and possible defeat for . . . [Lyon's] troops in battle will peril the continuing ascendancy of the Federal power itself, not only in the State, but in the whole West," the general admonished.

Lyon believed that if the interests of the Washington authorities were to be sustained in southwest Missouri as well as in the Mississippi Valley, large bodies of troops would have to be sent into Missouri. Lyon expressed strong opposition to Scott's plan to withdraw troops from the State. Troops hailing from the Mississippi Valley, Lyon observed, had already been rushed to the east. The general felt certain, "The moral effect of the presence of the few regulars in my command is doubtless the main consideration that holds the enemy in check, and with them I may be able to retain what

Maj. Gen. John C. Frémont
Commander of the Department of the West

Frémont was Lyon's superior and repeatedly refused to give Lyon reinforcements. Frémont received considerable criticism for this after the Battle of Wilson's Creek.

5

Brig. Gen. Nathaniel Lyon
Commander of the Union Forces
at the Battle of Wilson's Creek

Dr. William A. Hammond, who knew Lyon at Fort Riley, Kans., described him as " . . . intolerant of opposition, prone to inject the most unpopular opinions at times and places when he knew they would be unwelcome; easily aroused to a degree of anger that was almost insane in its manifestations; narrow minded, mentally unbalanced, and yet with all this, honest to the core, truthful . . . , intelligent, generous to a fault with those he liked, absolutely moral, attentive to his duties, a strict disciplinarian, and that he was one to trust in emergencies with absolute confidence that he would always do what he said he would do, even though he gave up his life for his constancy."

has already been achieved until I am strengthened, but any dimunition will be imminently hazardous."[8]

When Montgomery Blair learned of Lyon's difficulties, he visited General Frémont in New York City. Blair laid Lyon's entreaties before Frémont. The general then sent a telegram, couched in feeble terms, to the War Department that "General Lyon calls for reinforcements."[9] Next, Blair appealed to his fellow members of the cabinet. Whereupon, General Scott (on July 18) ordered Frémont to proceed to his command without the benefit of a visit to Washington.[10] Frémont reached St. Louis on July 25 and issued a General Order formally assuming command of the Western Department.[11]

Almost as soon as Frémont reached St. Louis, Lyon started sending emissaries to meet with the department commander and brief him on the state of affairs in southwestern Missouri. In addition, these men were directed to impress on Frémont just how vital it was to rush reinforcements to Springfield. (Among the officers sent to St. Louis were Col. John S. Phelps, Maj. Bernard G. Farrar, and Capt. John S. Cavender.)

At his interview with Frémont, Phelps (who had been elected to Congress and was en route to Washington to attend the special session called by President Abraham Lincoln) reported that the troops in the Army of the West had "not been paid, and are rather dispirited." Furthermore, he continued, "they are badly off for clothing, and the want of shoes unfits them for marching." Phelps also reported that there was a crying need for efficient staff officers at the front and the interests of the government suffered for want of them. The colonel called Frémont's attention to the status of the 3-months' volunteers. If Lyon were to hold his position it would be necessary to replace these units with newly constituted regiments. "The safety of the State," Phelps warned, "is hazarded; orders from General Scott strip the entire West of regular forces, and increase the chance of sacrificing it." At this very moment, the congressman observed, all the newspapers contained accounts announcing that troops from all the Confederate States west of the Mississippi River were moving toward the northern border of Arkansas, intent on invading Missouri.[12]

In reply, Frémont stated that he did not believe that General Lyon was in as "desperate straits" as Phelps had represented. Frémont said that he was confident that Maj. Gen. Sterling Price and Brig. Gen. Benjamin McCulloch "could have nothing but an inconsiderable force, since the country in Southwestern Missouri was too poor to support a force of any formidable strength." In the opinion of the general, "Lyon could take care of himself." Frémont told Phelps that at the moment he didn't have any troops to spare.

Information reaching Frémont from Gov. Oliver P. Morton of Indiana indicated that a powerful Confederate amphibious force led by Brig. Gen. Gideon J. Pillow would soon be coming up the Mississippi River. Pillow's initial objectives were said to be Cairo, Ill., and Bird's Point, Mo. To prevent the loss of these two key ports, Frémont observed, would require the use of every available man in his department.[13]

Major Farrar's and Captain Cavender's conversations with General Frémont followed the same line as that of Congressman Phelps. Frémont assured Lyon's emissaries that 5,000 troops would be sent into southwestern Missouri as soon as the necessary orders could reach them. Unfortunately for Lyon, military operations in and around Cairo, Ill., were inaugurated by the Federals. The Cairo Expedition monopolized Frémont's attention. He seemed to forget completely about his promise to reinforce Lyon. It was August 4 before Frémont issued marching orders to the 3d Kansas Infantry and the 7th Missouri Infantry. Both the Kansas regiment which was stationed at Fort Leavenworth and the Missouri unit based at Boonville were directed to proceed to Springfield.[14]

In the meantime, other messengers had reached Frémont's St. Louis headquarters bearing fresh appeals from Lyon for assistance. On July 26, Schofield had written to Colonel Harding. Having heard of the Union defeat at First Manassas, the major expressed concern lest this setback should keep Lyon from getting the promised reinforcements. "If so," Schofield warned, "the next news will be of our defeat also."

After touching on the need for additional troops, Schofield turned to the acute shortage of supplies. He pointed out that the soldiers were in need of clothing, particularly shoes. At the moment, Schofield announced, "Many of the men are entirely barefooted, and hence unable to march."[15]

The next day (July 27), Lyon addressed another dispatch to Colonel Harding. Lyon, having learned that the situation in the northern part of Missouri had improved, inquired into the possibility of transferring several regiments from that area into the southwestern part of the State. The general wanted Harding to "urge this matter upon Frémont, as of vital importance." Lyon expressed the opinion that the 3-months' volunteers would reenlist if they could be paid. He also pointed out that his army had been unable to move because of an acute shortage of supplies. This delay, Lyon reported, would exhaust the term of service of the 3-months' men. Lyon observed, "If the Government cannot give due attention to the West, her interests must have a corresponding disparagement."[16]

Frémont had proceeded to Cairo to give his personal attention to operations in that sector. Col. John C. Kelton, Frémont's chief of staff, was left in charge of the St. Louis headquarters. Evidently growing exasperated by the numerous messages reaching St. Louis from the Army of the West, Kelton (on August 2) telegraphed Frémont, "General Lyon wants soldiers — soldiers — soldiers!"[17]

Following Frémont's return to St. Louis, one of Lyon's couriers told the general that Lyon would fight at Springfield anyway. "If he fights," replied Frémont, "he will do it upon his own responsibility."[18]

Unable to obtain any reinforcements from Frémont, Lyon sought to recruit troops locally for the Federal service. He issued commissions to officers in the Home Guard companies and mustered in enlisted men. The general was visited by Union men from counties as much as 75 miles to the north and to the east of Springfield.[19]

In the meantime, General Lyon had learned from his scouts that the Confederates had occupied Forsyth, Mo. Accordingly, the general decided to send a strong task force to break up this Rebel concentration. Lyon, on July 19, issued a general order organizing and placing General Sweeny in charge of the Union command that would attack Forsyth.[20]

Sweeny's task force (consisting of artillery, cavalry, and infantry) left Springfield on the evening of July 20. Despite the rainy weather, Sweeny's 1,200 hardy men pushed grimly ahead. It took the Federals 2 days to cover the 45 miles of rugged countryside that lay between Springfield and Forsyth. By 6 p.m. on July 22, Sweeny's column had penetrated to within 3½ miles of its objective. At this point, Sweeny's advance guard (Company I, 2d Kansas Infantry [Mounted]) was challenged by several Rebel pickets. Pressing forward, the Kansans captured two of the Missourians before they could escape. When questioned by General Sweeny, the prisoners stated "that there were only 150 men stationed at Forsyth." This information caused Sweeny to decide to attack immediately. The general accordingly called for Capt. David S. Stanley of the cavalry. Stanley was directed to take his two companies of regulars and the mounted Kansans and surround the town.[21]

As soon as the cavalry disappeared down the road and before the remainder of Sweeny's task force tramped up, one of the captives changed his story. He told the general, "If that is all you have [referring to Stanley's cavalry], you will get badly whipped, for we have a thousand men in Forsyth. Although this statement was in contradiction to the one which the Southerner had made earlier, Sweeny was afraid that it might be true. He, therefore, sent a courier thundering forward with a message for Stanley "to keep the enemy in check if he found the resistance formidable, while . . . [Sweeny] hastened forward with the artillery and infantry to his support."[22]

In the meantime, the Southerners had been warned of the Yankees' approach. Captain Jackson quickly turned out the approximately 150 State Guards who were quartered in the courthouse. Hastily taking position guarding the approaches to the square, the Missourians "opened a scattering fire" on Stanley's troopers as they came thundering into town. The bluecoats replied with "a well-directed volley." This caused the Southerners to disperse. Evacuating Forsyth, the Rebels fled into the surrounding hills. Once they had reached the protection afforded by the trees and underbrush southwest of Forsyth, the State Guards commenced to snipe at the Federals. By this time, the Union artillery had arrived upon the scene. Unlimbering their two guns, the cannoneers of Battery F, 2d U. S. Light Artillery, began to hammer the hillsides where the Missourians were holed up with shell and canister. Unable to cope with the Union artillery, the State Guards ceased firing and vanished into the surrounding hills. By this time, Sweeny had deployed his infantry as skirmishers. Sweeping forward, the foot soldiers quickly mopped up the woods adjoining the town.[23]

Once his troops had secured Forsyth, Sweeny permitted them to camp. The officers then called the rolls. It was discovered that the capture of Forsyth had cost the Federals two men, both wounded. In addition, four horses had been killed, including Captain Stanley's. As expected, the State Guard made no report of their casualties. General Sweeny announced, "From the best information . . . [he] could gather, the loss of the enemy in killed was 8 or 10, and in wounded must have been several times that number. Among the dead was Captain Jackson, who took an active part in the skirmish." The Federals also reported that they had captured three of the Southerners.[24]

Sweeny's task force occupied Forsyth for about 18 hours. At noon on July 23, after the general had disposed of all the captured public property, he prepared to return to Springfield. Except for the capture of two Southerners, the return march was uneventful. Sweeny's task force entered Springfield at 2 p.m. on July 25. In less than 5 days, the Federals had marched 90 miles and fought one skirmish.[25]

On July 24, the day before Sweeny's task force returned from its raid on Forsyth, Lyon issued a General Order organizing the Army of the West into four brigades. Maj. Samuel D. Sturgis was placed in charge of the 1st brigade; Col. Franz Sigel had the 2d; Lt. Col. George L. Andrews commanded the 3d; Col. George W. Deitzler led the 4th.[26]

The shortage of supplies caused many of Lyon's troops to begin plundering. Reports of the wanton destruction of property and the disregard of personal rights began to flow into Lyon's headquarters. In an effort to stop these unauthorized depredations, Lyon issued a strongly worded General Order on July 26. He announced, "The persons and property of all law-abiding citizens will not be molested." Furthermore, Lyon intended that "this exemption shall apply to all persons, whatever may be their private opinions, who remain peaceful and quietly pursue their avocations, and who do not take nor excite others to take an attitude of hostility to the General Government." Individuals who were "exciting others to acts of rebellion," and were themselves in arms against the Federal Government, Lyon warned, might lose their property. He observed that the seizure of the property belonging to active secessionists would "be made only upon proper authority, and will have reference solely to the means of disarming and depriving them individually of power for mischief, and not to the injury of families or the wanton destruction of property."[27]

In the case of necessity, where private property had to be "seized or pressed into the use of the Army," it would have to be sanctioned by the commanding officer. Either the property would have to be paid for or a certificate of the seizure and a statement of the price due given.

Union Soldiers Foraging in Missouri

Foraging was a common way armies on both sides obtained their food supplies. The practice was cheap and convenient for the soldiers, but costly for civilians when they faced a hard winter without food.

Lyon announced that in the future he would "use all possible means to suppress" the wanton destruction of private property. He called upon all the officers and men, who were not guilty of these crimes, "to use all their exertions to this end." All the officers in the Army of the West were "enjoined to adopt the needful measures of vigilance and rigor to correct this evil."[28]

The next day (July 27), an excited courier galloped into Springfield with a message from Capt. Clark Wright. (The captain, who had established his headquarters at Greenfield, Mo., commanded the Dade County Mounted Home Guards.) Wright informed Lyon that one of his

A Game of Cards

Playing cards was the most common diversion soldiers on both sides pursued as they waited in their camp for orders.

scouts had just returned from the "southwest." The scout had informed Wright that Confederate troops were operating in the vicinity of Carthage, Sarcoxie, and Bowers' Mills as well as several other unidentified points. These troops, the scout reported, were apparently moving north. Questioning several of the Rebels, the spy learned that Brig. Gen. Benjamin McCulloch's command had marched east toward Cassville, Mo. In addition, he stated that Brig. Gen. James S. Rains' Missourians were moving on Springfield. The scout felt certain that the Confederates planned to attack Springfield from the west and south. If, however, Lyon sought to beat the Rebels to the punch by attacking first, the spy said the Southerners planned to receive the Federals "with masked batteries."

Wright informed Lyon that he was inclined to discount the intelligence concerning a Confederate drive on Springfield. He believed that these Rebel movements were designed to gather forage and collect provisions. To reinforce his opinion, Wright observed that the Confederates were "sweeping all before them as they advanced." On the previous day, 47 families driven from Carthage had passed through Greenfield. The refugees had given what Wright

13

described as "startling accounts of the depredations that are being committeed by the rebels as they return."

Wright also wrote Lyon that he had planted a spy in Rains' camp. When this man returned, the captain promised to give Lyon a full report.[29]

At 1 a.m. on July 28, an excited scout rode into Greenfield on a sweat-lathered horse. He informed Captain Wright that between 1,000 and 2,000 Confederates had left the Carthage area and were moving on Greenfield. To make matters worse, the scout reported that another 600 Rebels were at Sarcoxie, with 60 more at Bowers' Mill. These two forces, he stated, were also advancing toward Dade County. Upon the receipt of this distressing intelligence, Wright dashed off messages to General Lyon and Major Sturgis calling for reinforcements. (At this time, Sturgis' brigade was still encamped at Pond Springs.)[30]

When General Lyon received Captain Wright's urgent request for help, he issued instructions for a strong striking force to move to Greenfield. The column ordered to Wright's support consisted of five companies of the 1st Missouri, four companies of the 1st Kansas, and two of Sturgis' regular cavalry companies. If the Federals on reaching Greenfield found the Rebels too numerous to attack, the news would be immediately relayed to Lyon's headquarters. The Federals would then fall back, bringing with them the supplies which Wright's Home Guards had collected. If, however, the odds were such that the Northerners could give battle, they were to do so. After breaking up the Rebel force, the troops were to return to their camps.[31]

It was 43 long, hard miles from Springfield to Greenfield. Consequently, it was the morning of July 29 before the relief column reached Wright's camp. In the meantime, Wright had learned from his scouts that the Confederates, for the time being, had halted their advance. The emergency in Dade County having passed, the relief column retraced its steps.

Hardly had the troops returned from Dade County before a flood of reports reached Lyon's headquarters from his scouts. After evaluating these messages, Lyon concluded that the Rebels undoubtedly planned to converge on Springfield from three directions. While the main Confederate column moved up the Telegraph road from Cassville, supporting forces could be expected to march on Springfield

14

from Greenfield and Harrisonville. Lyon determined to try to beat the Confederates in detail. He accordingly massed his entire force in the Springfield area. The general proposed to wait until the Southerners had approached to with a 2-day march of his base. Lyon could then take the field and march against the main Rebel column. In the event that he was successful, the general would turn upon the other two.[32]

On August 1, Lyon learned from his scouts that a strong Rebel column was pushing up the Telegraph road. The general's informants told him that the Confederate vanguard was camped within 18 miles of Springfield. Lyon determined to put his plan into operation. He would attempt to beat the Southerners in detail. (Actually, Lyon had been misinformed about the Confederate plans. The Confederate forces had converged on Cassville, not Springfield, by three different roads. Lyon, however, did not know this. Misled by his scouts, the Union general continued to believe that the Southern columns would not unite until they had reached the Springfield area.) Lyon accordingly ordered his small army to take the field.[33]

Late on the afternoon of August 1, Lyon's column tramped out of Springfield. The Home Guards and a force of civilian volunteers were left to garrison the town. Ten miles southwest of Springfield, the troops forded Wilson Creek. The soldiers, after crossing the stream, halted and camped in the field north of Skegg's Branch. Here Lyon's column was joined by Sturgis' brigade and two foraging parties. (Sturgis' brigade had marched from Camp McClellan.) The addition of these commands increased Lyon's effective strength to 5,865 officers and men, supported by three batteries.[34]

The next morning the march was renewed. Capt. Frederick Steele with his infantry battalion and Battery F, 2d U. S. Light Artillery, spearheaded the Union advance. Soon after they had forded Terrell Creek, Steele's troops caught their first view of a mounted Confederate patrol. The Rebels were about 100 yards to their front. Steele immediately deployed two of his companies as skirmishers. These troops took position on either side of the Telegraph road. Meanwhile, Capt. James Totten had his gunners unlimber one of their six pieces. On shell from the gun sufficed; the Rebels scattered. A wagon partially loaded with cooked provisions was abandoned by the Southerners. The Yankees eagerly appropriated these welcomed rations.

Steele then recalled his skirmishers and the advance was resumed. Several miles were covered before Steele's bluecoats again caught a glimpse of the foe. This time, the Southerners began to snipe away at cavalrymen who were screening the left flank of Steele's battalion. Steele again deployed two of his companies, one to the left and the other to the right of the road. Confronted by the grim regulars, the mounted Southerners beat a hasty retreat.

As soon as he had reassembled his skirmishers, Steele again pushed ahead. The Federal vanguard, after advancing about 1½ miles, sighted a large number of Confederate cavalrymen crossing and recrossing the road to their front. The Telegraph road at that point ascended a steep hill. Steele's soldiers were unable to see the top of the hill because it was covered by a dense forest.

General Lyon now joined Captain Steele. The general decided against an immediate attack. This decision was forced on the general by several considerations. First, there was the terrain. On the right of the Telegraph road was a deep ravine, running at right angles to the road. From behind the hills, on the general's left, was a deep gulch leading toward the Confederates' position. The road was flanked on the left by the bed of a dry creek which was skirted by thick underbrush. As a result of the configuration of the ground, it was impossible for the general to obtain an accurate estimate of the Rebels' strength. Second, most of the Union troops had held up poorly on the march; there had been much straggling. Lyon attributed this to the fact that for nearly 3 weeks his men, except for a plentiful supply of meat, had been on less than half rations. Consequently, many of the soldiers were suffering from diarrhea. In addition, many of the volunteers were badly disciplined and poorly clothed. Finally, the day had been hot and the troops were suffering severely from the dust, the heat, and excessive thirst. At this time of the year, most of the springs and wells were dry. Toward evening on August 2, $5 was the asking price for "a canteen of warm ditch water." Lyon, therefore, ordered his troops to return to Dug Springs, where they camped.[35]

Before riding to Dug Springs, Lyon told Steele he was to hold his advance "position unless too hotly pressed by the enemy." If this eventuality came to pass, Steele was to fight a delaying action and fall back. At this point, the Telegraph road passed through a narrow valley at the end of which could be seen the Confederate horsemen. To the left of the road was a succession of spurs, sparsely covered with scrub oak. These spurs lay at right angles to the road. Steele deployed Company E, 2d U. S. Infantry, along the crest of "the last spur." The company of general service recruits commanded by Lt. Warren L. Lothrop was posted on the spur in the rear of Company E. Lance-Sgt. John Morine's company of Rifle Recruits was deployed as skirmishers in a cornfield on the right of the road. Company B, 2d U. S. Infantry, constituted Steele's reserve. Captain Stanley's cavalry was stationed a short distance in the rear of Steele's battalion.[36]

**Brig. Gen. Benjamin McCulloch,
Commander of Confederate Troops in
Arkansas and the Indian Territory**

After the incident with Rains' Division at Dug Springs, McCulloch never did trust the fighting abilities of the Missourians. McCulloch considered Price's Missourians to be a crude, undisciplined mob not worthy of associating with his troops. The tensions between Price and McCulloch never ceased.

**Brig. Gen. N. Bart Pearce, C.S.A.
Commander of the Arkansas State Troops**

II/Engagement at Dug Springs and the Confederate Concentration at Wilson Creek*

The news that General Lyon had reached Springfield was not long delayed in reaching the Confederates. During the third week of July, Brig. Gen. Benjamin McCulloch's brigade was camped in Benton County, Ark. (McCulloch's cantonment was located on Little Sugar Creek, adjacent to the Telegraph road.) On July 18, McCulloch wrote a long letter to the Confederate Secretary of War, Leroy P. Walker. He informed Walker that Lyon had reached Springfield with additional troops. The arrival of these newcomers had swelled the Union force at Springfield to between 9,000 and 10,000 mén, McCulloch wrote. At the moment, he pointed out, the Federals were busy fortifying Springfield. The general expressed the opinion that all the Federal forces in the southern part of Missouri "have concentrated at Springfield, and will be busily engaged for some time in strengthening that place."

McCulloch observed that he was eager to march against the Springfield Federals. He wrote that "if all the available forces now near me could be depended upon I think we could meet with success, or at least cut them [Lyon's troops] off entirely from their supplies and re-enforcements . . ." McCulloch informed Walker that he had already contacted the commander of the Missouri State Guard, General Price, on this subject. Price had told McCulloch that his force of between 8,000 and 9,000 men was "badly organized, badly armed, and now almost entirely out of ammunition." Under these circumstances, McCulloch observed, he did not think that the Missourians were disposed to take the offensive until they are better prepared.

---

* The U. S. Geological Survey uses the form "Wilson Creek" on its maps.

Next, McCulloch discussed the condition of the other Southern commands operating in the area. He reported that Brig. Gen. N. Bart Pearce's division of Arkansas State Troops was at Camp Walker, near Maysville, Ark. At this time, Pearce had about 2,200 officers and men. The Seventh Division of the Missouri State Guard commanded by Brig. Gen. James H. McBride was operating northwest of McCulloch's camp in Missouri. McCulloch greatly exaggerated McBride's strength when he listed his command as numbering about 2,000 strong. If these forces were properly armed and supplied with ammunition, McCulloch expressed the belief that "by rapid concentration we could drive the Federals out of Springfield, release the secession prisoners now there, and give our friends a chance of rallying around us."

"At present," McCulloch cautioned, "the condition of the Missouri forces will not warrant me in marching with my small command." Accordingly, he had taken up a strong position behind Little Sugar Creek. Here, he proposed to wait until the Missourians were ready to act.[1]

Within the week, however, McCulloch had a change of heart. To enable the Missourians to take the field, McCulloch decided to supply them with all the ammunition he could spare. Pearce also made available to the Missourians all the surplus ammunition that was stored in his magazines. Before taking the field, McCulloch insisted that Price agree to leave his unarmed men and camp followers behind. Price promised that these people would be left behind when the State Guard took the field. With this business taken care of, McCulloch designated Cassville, Mo., as the concentration point for the Rebel forces then operating in southwestern Missouri and northwestern Arkansas.[2]

The Missouri State Guard had spent the past several weeks camped on the Cowskin Prairie in MacDonald County. Much of the time since the battle of Carthage had been spent by the Missouri officers in drilling, organizing, and recruiting their commands. Price's troops, on July 25, started for Cassville. The Missourians reached the rendezvous on Sunday, July 28.[3]

McCulloch's brigade reached Cassville the day after the Missourians. Riding over to Price's camp, McCulloch was shocked to discover that the Missourian had not left his unarmed men and camp followers behind. Of the 9,000 to

10,000 men who were present in Price's camp, McCulloch estimated that the effective force would hardly reach 7,000. Furthermore, he was distressed to discover that nearly all the Missourians were "armed with shot-guns and common rifles." When McCulloch protested to Price on his violation of the agreement to leave the unarmed men and camp followers behind, Price remarked that they would be left at Cassville. He also asked McCulloch to "draw up the plan detailing the order of march upon Springfield."[4]

Pearce's troops, which had the greatest distance to march to reach Cassville, arrived on July 31. In the meantime, General McBride's division of the Missouri State Guard had reported to Price.

When he wrote to Secretary of War Walker on July 30, McCulloch announced that there were about 12,700 armed Confederates concentrated in and around Cassville. While the Missourians were indifferently armed, McCulloch observed that Pearce's infantry was "well armed." In addition, the general announced that his brigade, about 3,200 strong, were nearly all "well armed." McCulloch informed Walker that he would "move toward Springfield as rapidly as possible with the entire force, and hope soon to put the Missourians again in possession of it."[5]

McCulloch also told Walker that he had informed the commander of the District of Upper Arkansas, Brig. Gen. William J. Hardee, of his plans. At the same time, McCulloch had suggested to Hardee that it would be helpful if his command made a demonstration toward Rolla.[6]

On the afternoon of July 30, McCulloch issued instructions for the army to be ready to move out "as early as practicable." The Telegraph road would serve as the army's line of march. The advance contingents (the advance guard and the First Division) were alerted to be ready to take the field in the morning. Six mounted companies of Brig. Gen. James S. Rains' Eighth Division of the Missouri State Guard would spearhead the Confederates' advance. Rains was given the task because many of his men hailed from this section of Missouri and were familiar with the area. The advance guard would "habitually" keep about 10 miles ahead of the infantry. Four companies of cavalry were detailed to watch the flanks of the column. These flankers would be responsible to Rains.[7]

The army would march in three divisions. General McCulloch's "First Division" would have the lead. In addition to the 3d Louisiana and the 3d Arkansas Battalion, McCulloch's command included Col. John R. Gratiot's 3d Arkansas Infantry and Col. Richard H. Weightman's brigade of the Missouri State Guard. McCulloch's column would be accompanied by the Fort Smith Arkansas Battery. The "Second Division" was led by General Pearce. In addition to the artillery and infantry units assigned to Pearce's division of the Arkansas State Guard, the Second Division included all the infantry and artillery belonging to the Missouri State Guard, except for Weightman's brigade. Pearce's division was scheduled to leave Cassville on August 1. Since the greater portion of the Missouri State Guard marched in the Second Division, General Price accompanied General Pearce's command. The "Third Division," which would include all the mounted units attached to the army (except for those assigned to the advance guard and duty as flankers), would march from Cassville on August 2. Brigadier General Steele* of the Missouri State Guard commanded this division.[8]

In accordance with his agreement with McCulloch, Price issued orders dealing with his unarmed men and camp followers. It was announced on July 30 that, "All persons now in the army, but not forming part of it, and all unarmed men, must keep at least one day's march in the rear of the Third Division."[9]

Hardly had McCulloch left Cassville before Price changed his mind. On July 31, Price issued a General Order countermanding the one requiring that the unarmed organized companies of the Missouri State Guard keep one day's march in the rear of the Third Division. Instead, all dismounted organized companies were alerted to march in the rear of Pearce's division; the mounted units were to ride behind the Third Division. The status of the unarmed men who had not been mustered into State service remained unchanged. They would continue to travel a day's march in the rear of the army. Since General Steele was absent, Brig. Gen. Alexander E. Steen was placed in charge of the Third Division. [10]

---

* Sources readily available to the Missouri State Historical Society and Mr. Bearss fail to list Steele's first name and middle initial.

The First and Second Divisions marched as scheduled. By the evening of August 1, McCulloch's division had reached Crane Creek. Here, his troops camped for the night. At the same time, Pearce's command bivouacked on Flat Creek. Early the next morning, McCulloch received a message from Rains stating that his advance guard was in contact with a strong force of Yankees. McCulloch relayed this message to General Price, who was traveling with Pearce's command. McCulloch also stated that it was his intention to remain at Crane Creek until he had been joined by the Second and Third Divisions.

Upon receipt of this dispatch, General Price directed Pearce to McCulloch's assistance. Price also issued orders for Steen's Third Division to hasten to the point of danger. "Old Pap" accompanied Pearce's command as it tramped up the Telegraph road. Pearce's troops reached McCulloch's Crane Creek encampment during the forenoon. It was late in the afternoon before Steen's mounted division reached the Crane Creek area. Since most of the good camping sites were already occupied, Steen's troopers camped at a spring 3 miles south of Crane Creek.[11]

When Pearce's division put in an appearance, McCulloch was shocked to discover that the unarmed Missourians had accompanied the expedition. The first group of unarmed men that McCulloch sighted stated that they belonged to Brig. Gen. John B. Clark's Third Division of the Missouri State Guard. McCulloch urged Clark to send these men back. To reinforce his arguments, McCulloch pointed out that they would consume supplies destined for the fighting men. Furthermore, there was the danger that the unarmed men and camp followers would panic in case of a battle. Clark, however, refused to listen to McCulloch's plea. To make matters worse, he lacked the authority to enforce his wishes.[12]

Rains' outposts had established contact with Lyon's vanguard on the morning of August 2. The Missourians had fallen back when fired on by one of Totten's guns. Rains, upon being informed of this development, immediately relayed the news to General McCulloch. Rains assembled his command (about 400 strong) and moved to engage the Federals. As they descended into a valley about 3 miles from their camp, Rains' Missourians sighted Steele's bluecoats. The timber and underbrush prevented the Rebels from obtaining an accurate picture of the Federals' strength.

During the afternoon, there were several brief clashes between Rains' outposts and the Union scouts.[13]

When McCulloch learned that Rains' advance guard was in contact with the foe, he called for his adjutant, Col. James McIntosh. The colonel was told to take 150 men and ascertain the strength and position of the Federals. Leaving Crane Creek at the head of his combat patrol, McIntosh hastened up the Telegraph road. After a 7-mile ride, McIntosh encountered Rains' adjutant. The staff officer told the colonel that Rains "was engaging the enemy in front." Before proceeding any farther, McIntosh had his men take cover on either side of the road. Accompanied by the adjutant, the colonel then proceeded to the front. When the colonel reached Rains' command post, the general told him that "the enemy were immediately in front." McIntosh was unable to see any Yankees. He, therefore, told the general that he did not believe the foe was present in force. McIntosh, however, was not satisfied with the view from the command post. He rode forward to make a personal reconnaissance. From the top of a commanding hill, the colonel was able to obtain "a good view of the road in advance, and saw either a train or an encampment near it."

Rejoining Rains, McIntosh told him what he had seen. The colonel stated that, in his opinion, there were not more than 150 Yankees in front of Rains' advance guard. Before returning to Crane Creek, McIntosh informed Rains that he was not to attack the Northerners. Rains' mission was to see if he could discover the foe's position and strength. At dusk, Rains' Missourians were to fall back and take up a strong defensive position. If Rains were attacked, McIntosh promised that McCulloch would send reinforcements. This business taken care of, McIntosh assembled his patrol and retraced his steps.[14]

Rains' troopers, during the afternoon, succeeded in emplacing two mountain howitzers on either side of the road. With their two little guns, they sought to annoy the Federals. None of the shots, however, took effect. About 5 p.m., Rains' Missourians, despite McIntosh's instructions, launched a sharp thrust on the left flank and front of Company E, 2d U. S. Infantry. The commander of the regulars, Sgt. G. H. McLaughlin, estimated that he was attacked by 400 Rebels, half of whom were mounted. Moments later, a second Confederate column, accompanied by the two mountain howitzers, was sighted advancing along the Telegraph road. McLaughlin's regulars beat off the initial Rebel thrust. Quickly re-forming, the Missourians (spearheaded by Col. Jesse L. Craven's regiment) renewed the attack. This time, McLaughlin's infantrymen were forced to retire on Lieutenant Lothrop's command. The two companies then fell back into the road. By this time, Captain Steele had moved to the front with the two other companies of his battalion. Pressing forward, the regulars beat the Missourians back a second time.[15]

In the meantime, Captain Stanley had committed his troopers. The Union cavalryman took his position on a commanding spur to the left and front of Steele's battalion. Stanley's regulars then charged and cut a swath through the Confederate line. The Rebels fell back. As they pressed forward, Steele's infantry sighted an estimated 200 horses tied in a ravine and apparently abandoned by the retreating Missourians. Before the Yankees could secure the mounts, they were recalled by General Lyon.[16]

The U. S. Cavalry Charge at Dug Springs

Capt. David S. Stanley led a cavalry charge against Rains' Division of the Missouri State Guard and put them to flight. This was the only significant contact Lyon had made with the elusive Southerners during the day the Union force spent at Dug Springs.

When Rains discovered that the Yankees were retiring, he took heart. Colonel Cravens' regiment was sent to attack Stanley's cavalry which was covering Steele's withdrawal. Simultaneously, Rains took the remainder of his command and sought to cut off the Union cavalry. A messenger was also sent galloping to inform McIntosh that the advance guard was "engaged with a large force." By this time, Lyon had formed his command into line of battle. A section of six-pounder guns belonging to the 1st Battery of Backoff's battalion and the six pieces manned by the cannoneers of Battery F had been placed in battery. Captain Totten waited until the Southerners had approached to within 600 yards before directing his men to open fire. The gun captains then pulled the lanyards. This caused the Missourians to scatter. Rains reported that a portion of his command "became panic-stricken and retired in the utmost confusion."[17]

Before he reached Crane Creek, McIntosh was overtaken by Rains' command. In his report of the affair, McIntosh wrote that Rains' command, "as . . . [he] expected, came down upon us in full flight and in the greatest confusion." To curb the panic, McIntosh deployed his men astride the road. The fresh troops were able to partially arrest the rout. Shortly before the first of the stragglers appeared, Rains' messenger had thundered up. When informed that Rains had attacked the bluecoats and needed reinforcements, McIntosh, having no disposition to sacrifice his small command, declined to march to his comrade's assistance.[18]

In spite of McIntosh's efforts, a large number of Rains' troops did not stop running until after they had crossed Crane Creek. Capt. William E. Woodruff, a member of the Pulaski Battery, recalled:

> A few minutes later [The battery had just gone into camp.] occurred a moving scene. Gen. Rains' unattached Missourians in seeming hordes, came rushing south across the ford at Crane Creek, with any imaginable numbers and style of vehicle and people, mounted and on foot.[19]

Casualties in the skirmish at Dug Springs had been trifling. General Rains reported that he lost one officer and five men wounded; the Federals listed their losses as about 36 wounded, most of them slightly, and five dead. Another aspect, however, served to give this engagement considerable importance. The conduct of Rains' troops on this occasion (which was derisively dubbed "Rains' Scare") caused McCulloch to lose all confidence in the Missouri State Guards. Here were planted the seeds of the distrust and ill-feeling which eventually separated the combined armies and frustrated the Confederate hopes for recovering Missouri.[20]

Writing of the engagement at Dug Springs to Secretary of War Judah P. Benjamin in December, McCulloch reported:

> It was at this point I first saw the total inefficiency of the Missouri mounted men under Brigadier-General Rains. A thousand, more or less, of them composed the advance guard, and whilst reconnoitering the enemy's position, some 8 miles distant from our camp, were put to flight by a single cannon-shot, running in the greatest confusion, without the loss of a single man except one, who died of overheat or sun-stroke, and bringing no reliable information as to the position or force of the enemy; nor were they of the slightest service as scouts or spies afterwards.[21]

The next day (August 3), Lyon's Army of the West resumed its advance. At Curran Post Office, 3 miles beyond Dug Springs, the Federals encountered a small Confederate patrol. These Confederates had moved across country from Marion and were busy preparing their dinner when the Union vanguard popped into view. A few shots from Totten's battery sufficed to scatter the Rebels. After occupying the Southerners' camp, Lyon permitted his men to camp. The 2d Kansas then advanced 2 miles farther to McCulla's Springs without seeing any additional signs of the foe.[22]

Lyon's army remained at Curran Post Office, with the 2d Kansas thrown forward to McCulla's Springs, for about 20 hours. The Union general was disappointed when his scouts were unable to pinpoint the main Confederate force. Lyon, however, had received reports that a large force of Missourians were moving to Price's support from the direction of Sarcoxie. Furthermore, Lyon was afraid that the Rebels might utilize their cavalry to cut him off from his base at Springfield. To make matters worse, supplies were getting scarce. Lyon, therefore, called a council of war. He laid before the assembled officers the question of whether they should advance or retreat. Next, the general expounded at length on "the possible and probable consequences" of the two alternatives which were open to the enemy. Lyon then asked the opinion of each of the officers present. The question was freely debated. All seemed willing "to risk a pitched battle," if one could be fought before the army's supplies were exhausted. But it was decided that, under the existing circumstances, there was nothing left to do but retire.[23]

With the decision to fall back having been made, Lyon addressed a letter to General Frémont. After describing the advance to Curran Post Office, Lyon wrote of his determination to fall back. The general informed his superiors that he had reports indicating that the Rebels were trying to bypass his army and beat him into Springfield. Lyon hoped that the Home Guards and civilian volunteers would be able to hold the city until his return. Lyon wrote that even if he reached Springfield first, he doubted that he would be able to hold the city. Furthermore, he believed that the numerically superior Confederate cavalry would keep his army from drawing flour from the mills of the area.

Then, to make matters worse, Lyon's army was about to start melting away. The term of enlistment for the infantrymen of the 1st Iowa expired on August 14. At various times in the period between August 9 and 18, the companies in the 5th Missouri would be able to claim their discharge. A large percentage of the 3d Missouri would also be mustered out during the same period. Lyon observed that the discharge of these troops would reduce his command "to about 3,500 men, badly clothed and without prospect of supplies." The discouraged general pointed out:

> Prudence seems now to indicate the necessity of withdrawing, if possible, from the county, and falling [back] upon either St. Louis or Kansas. Saint Louis via Rolla will most likely be selected, with a view to re-enforcements and supplies.[24]

Next, Lyon reported on the Confederate strength. The general observed that he was sure that he was confronted by 15,000 Rebels. If the Southerners sought to isolate his army, Lyon believed they might be able to increase their striking forces to 20,000. Most of these, Lyon admitted, would "be ill-conditioned troops, collected from Missouri and Arkansas, with such fire-arms as each man may have . . ." In addition to these men, the Confederate were reported to have available McCulloch's command. (At this time, Lyon did not know that McCulloch and Price had joined forces.) Lyon reported that McCulloch was supposed to have 4,000 soldiers, "well-armed, and prepared for effective service."[25]

On the morning of August 4, Lyon's army started for Springfield. It took the Federal column the greater part of 2 days to complete the 24-mile march. The soldiers bivouacked on the night of August 4 on Terrell Creek, where Moody's Spring furnished an abundant supply of fresh water. When the army reached Springfield, on the afternoon of August 5, Lyon had most of his men camp in and around the town. About 2,000 regulars and volunteers commanded by Colonel Andrews and Major Sturgis were posted 4 miles southwest of Springfield on the Telegraph road.[26]

The Confederate army remained in the Crane Creek area on August 3. During the night, the Rebel force was strengthened by the arrival of the hard-riding South Kansas-Texas Regiment commanded by Col. Elkanah Greer.[27]

While the two armies confronted each other (the Confederates at Crane Creek and the Yankees at Curran Post Office), General Price approached General McCulloch and "begged" him to attack. McCulloch, however, had been disillusioned by the Missourians' conduct at Dug Springs. He had made up his mind not to cooperate with the Missourians any longer. McCulloch refused to advance any farther. He gave as his reason the excuse that the Confederate government had refused to grant him authority to move into Missouri except to afford protection to the Indian Territory. If he pushed any farther into Missouri, McCulloch observed, the security of the Indian Territory might be jeopardized and he would find himself subject to the censure of his government.[28]

While this was a good excuse for not seizing the initiative, it was not McCulloch's real reason for refusing to attack Lyon. McCulloch simply had no confidence in the Missouri State Guard nor did the general have any faith in Price's skill as an officer. Furthermore, with the exception of Colonel Weightman, McCulloch had a profound contempt for the ability of the Missouri officers. McCulloch had disliked Rains from the beginning. Now he was further embittered against Rains, because of the open quarrel which had broken out between the Jasper County politician and Colonel McIntosh following the engagement at Dug Springs. Since McIntosh was a graduate of the United States Military Academy, McCulloch had a high opinion of his abilities. Neither McCulloch nor McIntosh were able to discern the qualities in Price which endeared "Old Pap"

Maj. Gen. Sterling Price
Commander of the Missouri State Guard

In Albert Castel's words, Price "displayed a laxness in enforcing discipline, a tendency to quarrel with other officials, and a penchant for acting in a highly independent, almost insubordinate fashion . . ."

to his troops. They could not be made to believe " 'the undisciplined mob' which Price commanded would under his eyes fight as well as the veterans of Wellington or Napoleon ever fought." Confronted by McCulloch's resolute refusal to advance, Price returned to his quarters.[29]

The next morning (August 4), Price, accompanied by his adjutant (Thomas L. Snead), once more called upon General McCulloch. Price again asked McCulloch to attack Lyon. McCulloch refused for a second time to take the offensive. Price, who had a "loud voice and positive address," always spoke to McCulloch as if the latter were his inferior. Raising his voice, Price demanded, "Do you mean to march on and attack Lyon, Gen. McCulloch?"

"I have not received orders yet to do so, sir," answered McCulloch, "my instructions leave me in doubt whether I will be justified in doing so."

Price, in a loud, imperious tone, said:

Now, sir, I am an older man than you, Gen. McCulloch, and I am not only your senior in rank now, but I was a brig-gen in the Mexican War, with an independent command, when you were only a captain; I have fought and won more battles than you have ever witnessed; my force is twice as great as yours; and some of my officers rank, and have seen more service than you, and we are also upon the soil of our own state; but, Gen. McCulloch, if you will consent to help us whip Lyon and to repossess Missouri, I will put myself and all my forces under your command, and we will obey you as faithfully as the humblest of your own men. We can whip Lyon, and we will whip him and drive the enemy out of Missouri, and all the honor and all the glory shall be yours. All that we want is to regain our homes and to establish the independence of Missouri and the South. If you refuse to accept this offer, I will move with the Missourians alone, against Lyon. For it is better that they and I should all perish than Missouri be abandoned without a struggle. You must either fight beside us, or look on at a safe distance, and see us fight all alone the army which you dare not attack even with our aid. I must have your answer before dark, for I intend to attack Lyon to-morrow.[30]

As Price was speaking, McCulloch suddenly recalled that his chief commissary had told him that the army was short of food. At this time, the supply of breadstuffs had almost given out. McCulloch felt that the reason behind Price's proposition was a desire to throw upon his shoulders the responsibility for ordering a retreat. To stall for time, McCulloch informed the Missourian that he was expecting dispatches from the East. In any case, he would make his decision known to Price before sundown.[31]

In the meantime, General Price had called his officers together and told them what he had done. They were at first violently opposed to Price's action. Nevertheless, they were finally prevailed upon to give "their unwilling consent to what they considered an unnecessary self-abasement."[32]

Before the designated hour, Maj. Andrew J. Dorn reached McCulloch's headquarters with a letter from Maj. Gen. Leonidas Polk. (At this stage of the conflict, Polk was in command of Department Number 2 with headquarters at Memphis, Tenn.) Polk informed McCulloch that General Pillow was advancing into Missouri at the head of 12,000 men. (Pillow's command was operating out of New Madrid, Mo.) This news forced McCulloch's hand. He decided to accept the command of the combined armies.[33]

Accompanied by McIntosh, McCulloch then hastened to Price's headquarters. After telling Price of the receipt of Polk's message, McCulloch announced that he had concluded to take command and would attack General Lyon. Price had Captain Snead draft an order announcing to his troops that he had turned over the command of the State Guard to General McCulloch. The Missouri general, however, reserved to himself the right to resume his command at his own pleasure.[34]

Believing that the Federals were still at Curran Post Office, McCulloch decided to make a night march. Orders were drafted, alerting the army to be ready to march at midnight. The crack 3d Louisiana, supported by the Pulaski Arkansas Battery, would constitute the vanguard. Next would come the infantry and the other attached batteries. The various infantry commands were slated to march in column by platoons. No cavalry or mounted men, with the exception of the officers, would be allowed in this portion of the column. The cavalry, riding in column of fours, would follow Price's artillery. As soon as the advance guard had established contact with the Yankees, Price would direct General Steen to move the Missouri cavalrymen into position on the left of the infantry; the other mounted units (the 1st and 2d Arkansas Mounted Rifles, the 1st Arkansas Cavalry, and the South Kansas-Texas Regiment) would be deployed to the right of the foot-soldiers. General Price was to take charge of the Confederate left wing after the army had been formed.[35]

Since McCulloch hoped to take the Federals by surprise, he ordered that the beating of drums and all unnecessary shouting be dispensed with. Before starting the day's march, the officers were to see that the canteens were filled. One day's ration (cooked) was carried by each man. No unarmed men or camp followers were to accompany the column. The regimental commanders were to detail men to guard their units' trains. To assist in identification, McCulloch and his aides would wear a white badge on each arm.

In an effort to boost morale, McCulloch had the adjutants read an order urging the soldiers "to look steadily to the front." They were reminded "that the eyes of our gallant brothers in arms, who have so nobly acquitted themselves in the East [referring to the battle of First Manassas], are upon you. They are looking for a second victory here. Let us move forward, then, with a common resolve to a glorious victory."[36]

The Confederate vanguard marched at the designated hour. McCulloch, as he rode along, informed his staff that he expected to launch a surprise attack on the Federal encampment at daybreak. Before the general had proceeded very far, however, he learned from his scouts that the Yankees had evacuated their camp at Curran Post Office about 20 hours before and were falling back on Springfield.

Undaunted by this news, the general decided to make a forced march in an effort to overtake Lyon's retreating army. Though the weather was blistering and the dust almost unendurable, the Rebels pushed on. Captain Woodruff of the Pulaski Battery remembered this march as:

> The hardest within recollection, the 1st day from Van Buren excepted. It was fearfully hot and the men were at the verge of exhaustion. The tired 3d Louisiana swarmed around the gun on the road, hoping and begging to ride. Our officers [the Pulaski Battery] were compelled to refuse — the teams had to be protected, and they were as tired as the Louisianians. The captain and lieutenants were the horses only friends.[37]

Not until the column had reached Moody's Spring did McCulloch permit a prolonged halt. By this time, the general realized that the Federals had escaped. Since there was a good supply of drinking water at the spring, McCulloch's troops bivouacked for the night on Terrell Creek. Captain Woodruff recalled that when the word to camp was passed, "the men all fell where they halted, and went to sleep where they lay, supperless; and it was only by personal exertion of the officers that the teams were unharnessed and picketed."[38]

Learning from his scouts that there were a number of fields of ripening corn several miles ahead at the point where the Telegraph road crossed Wilson Creek, McCulloch ordered the march renewed on the morning of August 6. As a result of a critical shortage of food supplies, this corn would be used to supplement the rations which the army carried.[39]

Before daybreak, Captain Woodruff received orders from army headquarters assigning his battery to the 3d Louisiana. The Louisianians and their supporting battery would again spearhead the army's advance. After disposing of the rations that were left in their haversacks, the Arkansas cannoneers limbered up their four pieces and moved to secure the position in the column. On doing so, they discovered that Capt. Hiram Bledsoe's three-gun Missouri Battery was trying to force its way into their place. Fortunately for the units involved, Colonel McIntosh rode up and succeeded in straightening out the misunderstanding. After this difficulty was settled, the advance was resumed. After a short march, the Confederates halted and went into camp on both sides of Wilson Creek.[40]

Wilson Creek has changed little since the Civil War. Now, as then, Wilson Creek rises in and around Springfield. The stream flows in a westerly direction for about 5 miles, before veering sharply to the south. About 9 miles beyond this point, the creek debouches into the James river, a tributary of the White. About 1 mile above its confluence with the James, Wilson Creek receives the waters of Terrell Creek, which comes in from the west. One and one-half miles above the mouth of Terrell Creek, Skegg's Branch discharges into Wilson Creek. Like Terrell Creek, Skegg's Branch flows from west to east. At the time of the war, the Telegraph road crossed both Terrell Creek and Skegg's Branch near their mouths. About ½-mile north of Skegg's Branch, the Telegraph road crossed Wilson Creek. Springfield lay about 10 miles northeast of this ford.

Bounded by Wilson Creek on the east, Terrell Creek on the south, and in part by the Telegraph road on the west were several large cornfields. Here, where there was a considerable belt of relatively level ground, most of the Confederate cavalry bivouacked. In addition to Col. Elkanah B. Greer's Texans, Col. Thomas J. Churchill's 1st Arkansas Mounted Rifles and Col. De Rosey Carroll's 1st Arkansas Cavalry, about 700 mounted Missourians belonging to Col.

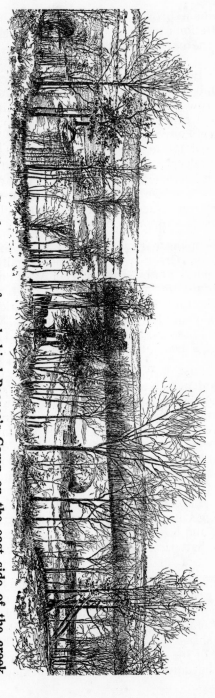

The Battlefield of Wilson Creek as seen from behind Pearce's Camp on the east side of the creek.

35

William Brown's regiment and Lt. Col. James P. Major's battalion camped in these fields. General Steen was in charge of the cavalry's encampment.[41]

Between Skegg's Branch and the ford where the Telegraph road crossed Wilson Creek, the valley was quite narrow. At this point, the road paralleled the west bank of the stream. West of the road rose a commanding eminence, since known as "Bloody Hill." The crest of the hill was almost 170 feet higher than the creek at this point; its sides were deeply scarred with ravines, and dented here and there with sinkholes. In 1861, as it is today, the hill was covered with a dense growth of underbrush and scrub oak. At numerous places on the hill, especially near its crest, there were outcroppings of rocks.

In the narrow valley between the foot of the hill and Wilson Creek were bivouacked all the infantry of the Missouri State Guard, except Weightman's brigade. Price's headquarters were next to the road, about 200 yards south of the ford. Brig. Gens. John B. Clark's, William Y. Slack's, Mosby M. Parsons', and James H. McBride's divisions of the Missouri State Guard occupied the ground between Price's headquarters and Skegg's Branch.[42]

East of Wilson Creek (opposite the area where Price's infantry had encamped) was a plateau. This ground was about 30 feet above the stream. The infantry and artillery assigned to Generals McCulloch's and Pearce's commands were encamped on this terrain. Captain Woodruff's Pulaski Battery was posted on a partially detached portion of the plateau near the Guinn house. Woodruff's gunners were given the mission of covering the approaches to the ford. Capt. J. G. Reid's Fort Smith Arkansas Battery camped at the southern edge of the plateau, opposite the mouth of Skegg's Branch. Pearce's three infantry regiments (the 3d, 4th, and 5th Arkansas) bivouacked in the area between the two batteries. Pearce's command post was located in the center of his division's encampment.[43]

The two infantry units belonging to McCulloch's brigade camped on the northwestern section of the plateau. Lt. Col. Dandridge McRae's battalion bivouacked on the left and the 3d Louisiana on the right. Colonel McIntosh's 2d Regiment, Arkansas Mounted Rifles, pitched their tents on the east side of the creek just above the ford. McCulloch established his headquarters near the Guinn house. Weightman's Missouri brigade was at Manley's Spring about ½-mile east of the encampment of the Fort Smith Battery.[44]

Col. James Cawthorn's mounted brigade of Rains' division camped in the ravine, which debouched into Wilson Creek from the west about ½-mile north of the ford. This ravine bounded "Bloody Hill" on the north. Rains' quarters, however, were on the opposite side of the creek at Gibson's Mill. A few of Rains' troopers also bivouacked on the left bank of Wilson Creek.[45]

Col. Benjamin A. Rives' cavalry regiment, which was attached to Slack's division of the Missouri State Guard, camped near the head of a ravine that scarred the south face of "Bloody Hill." This was several hundred yards southwest of the hollow where Cawthorn's troopers had bivouacked.[46]

While waiting for his supply trains to arrive, McCulloch called on the Missourians, who were presumably familiar with the area, for information regarding the Federals' strength and position. Price assured McCulloch that his scouts and spies would obtain the desired information. When the Missourians were unable to penetrate the Springfield defenses and obtain the desired data, McCulloch was exasperated. He decided to see if he personally could discover what Lyon's intentions were. Accordingly, McCulloch daily would sling his Maynard rifle across his shoulders and reconnoiter toward Springfield. Sometimes the general would be accompanied by a large patrol. At other times he would venture forth "almost alone." But adventurous, daring and skillful as he was, McCulloch was no more successful than the Missourians in ascertaining either Lyon's intentions or his strength. Moreover, he was unable to learn whether or not Lyon had fortified his position.[47]

When Price and the Missouri generals pleaded for him to resume the advance, McCulloch replied that he "would not make a blind attack upon Springfield." Calling Price's attention to the Missourians' failure to penetrate the Union outposts, McCulloch declared he "would order the whole army back to Cassville rather than bring on an engagement with an unknown enemy."[48]

On Thursday (August 8), Price finally received news from two "loyal" ladies. The two women had succeeded in obtaining from General Lyon permission to pass through the Union lines. Following a circuitous route by way of Pond Springs, the two ladies reached Price's headquarters. They informed Price "that Lyon was greatly perplexed; that he was in constant expectation of being attacked; that he had kept his men under arms all the time; and that he was getting ready to abandon Springfield." Visiting McCulloch, Price told him what he had just learned. After vouching for the credibility of his informants, Price again urged McCulloch to attack. McCulloch promised to consider the matter carefully and to let Price know his decision by evening. Accompanied by McIntosh and a number of scouts, McCulloch rode to the front. The hour was late when the general returned from his reconnaissance. Instead of letting Price know his decision regarding the projected attack, McCulloch retired to his quarters.[49]

Awakening at daybreak, Price called for Captain Snead. The irate Price told the staff officer to go to McCulloch's headquarters and ask him what he intended to do. Snead crossed Wilson Creek and hastened to McCulloch's tent. While the captain was talking with McCulloch, Price rode up. The Missourian's impatience was no longer controllable. He insisted "with great vehemence that McCulloch should keep the promise he had made at Crane Creek, and lead the army out against Lyon."[50]

To appease the thoroughly aroused Price, McCulloch agreed to meet all the general officers at Price's headquarters at noon. At this gathering, the officers would determine upon some plan of action. At the council of war, McCulloch expressed great unwillingness to attack the Springfield Federals. Price, however, "declared emphatically that if orders were not forthwith issued for a forward movement, he would resume command of the Missouri troops and himself give battle to Lyon, be the consequences what they might." Confronted by this ultimatum, McCulloch yielded. He issued orders for his subordinates to have their soldiers ready to march at 9 p.m. McCulloch proposed to have his command move in four columns (each converging on Springfield from a different direction) and attack the Federals at daylight on August 10.[51]

Once the orders to advance had been read to the men by the adjutants, the camps were thrown into a turmoil "of suppressed excitement." General Pearce recalled:

The scene of preparation, immediately following the orders so long delayed and now so eagerly welcomed by the men, was picturesque and animating in the extreme. The question of ammunition was one of the most important and serious, and as the Ordnance Department was imperfectly organized and poorly supplied, the men scattered about in groups, to improvise, as best they could, ammunition for their inefficient arms. Here, a group would be molding bullets — there, another crowd dividing percussion-caps, and, again, another group fitting new flints in their old muskets. They had little thought then of the inequalities between the discipline, arms, and accouterments of the regular United States troops they were soon to engage in battle, and their own homely movements and equipment. It was a new thing to most of them, this regular way of shooting by word of command, and it was, perhaps, the old-accustomed method of using rifle, musket, or shot-gun as gamesters or marksmen that won them the battle when pressed into close quarters with the enemy.[52]

About 9 p.m., just as the army was preparing to move, it started to sprinkle. Since it was dark and gloomy, McCulloch was afraid that this slight precipitation would be followed by a downpour. Before determining his next move, McCulloch conferred with Price. McCulloch informed the Missourian that the command had an average of only 25 rounds of ammunition per man. Furthermore, there was no more ammunition "short of Fort Smith or Baton Rouge." McCulloch pointed out that, "Not more than one man in four was furnished with anything better than bags made of cotton cloth in which to carry their cartridges." He observed that the slightest rain would almost disarm them, because "many of the men had nothing but the common shot-gun and rifle of the country, without bayonets." In view of these difficulties, McCulloch announced that he was countermanding the march. Instead, the officers would hold their men "in readiness to move whenever ordered." Price, realizing that a heavy rain would "virtually disarm" three-quarters of the Confederates, raised no objection to McCulloch's decision.[53]

The Confederates spent the night of August 9 lying on their arms, waiting for the order to advance. General Pearce remembered that:

The men did not "sulk in their tents," but rested on their arms in no amiable mood. This condition of uncertainty and suspense lasted well through the night, as the commanding officers were better informed than the men of the risks to be encountered, and of the probable result, in case they should make an aggressive fight against disciplined forces when only half prepared.[54]

At least one of the four artillery units attached to the Rebel army, the Pulaski Battery, kept their teams harnessed and hitched to the guns throughout the night. Before daybreak, the artillerists ate their breakfast, largely green corn, which they had gathered the previous afternoon.[55]

About dawn, General Price again sent Captain Snead across Wilson Creek, to see if he could learn what McCulloch proposed to do. McCulloch and McIntosh, upon conversing with Snead, decided to see Price. Fording the stream, the two officers (accompanied by Snead) hastened to Price's headquarters. Since Price's cook was about to serve a breakfast consisting of corn bread, lean beef, and coffee, McCulloch and McIntosh were invited to share it.

III/General Lyon Decides to Attack

When General Lyon returned to Springfield following the march to Curran Post Office, most of his Army of the West encamped about the city. Colonel Andrews and Major Sturgis with about 2,000 regulars and volunteers, however, were posted at Camp Hunter on the Telegraph road 4 miles southwest of Springfield. To guard against a surprise attack and prevent news of his plans and strength from reaching the Confederates, Lyon moved to seal off the city. A close watch was kept on all the roads leading into town. Although the Union sentries permitted anyone to enter the city, no one was allowed to go out except physicians, who first had to present passes signed by the military.[1]

General Lyon consulted freely with his officers and the leading Union men of Springfield following his return to the city. The general clearly saw the developing strategic situation. His scouts kept him constantly informed of the Rebels' movements. Lyon said that he was "impatient to fight" McCulloch's command, but he anxiously desired reinforcements to enable him to have a reasonable chance of success. Every day he visited his outposts and sent off pleas for assistance. At times, Lyon would lose his temper and curse and swear violently. Two prominent Union men of Greene County recalled one incident when Lyon received a dispatch from Frémont stating that no more troops could or would be sent for the present. As the general strode back and forth in his room, with the paper in his hand, he suddenly threw it on the table, and clapping his hands together, cried out **"G-d d--n General Frémont:** He is a worse enemy to me and the Union cause than Price and McCulloch and the whole d----d tribe of rebels in this part of the State!"[2]

On the afternoon of August 6, Lyon learned from his spies that the Confederate vanguard was encamped on Wilson Creek. He, therefore, decided to make a night attack on this force with a portion of Colonel Andrews' and Major Sturgis' brigades. Andrews and Sturgis were alerted to have their men in ranks and the artillery horses harnessed by 6 p.m. In the meantime, scouts were sent out to reconnoiter the Confederate position.[3]

Shortly after Lyon had issued the marching orders to Andrews and Sturgis, a report reached the general stating that a Union patrol consisting of two companies of Home Guards led by Capt. Job B. Stockton had clashed with a party of Price's cavalry on the Grand Prairie, west of town. In this engagement, two of the Home Guard had been wounded. Two companies were immediately ordered to Stockton's support. Simultaneously, eight companies of the 1st Kansas, part of the 2d Kansas, and Maj. Peter J. Osterhaus' battalion were turned out. Lyon proposed to use these units to support Andrews' and Sturgis' attack on the Confederate advance guard. The hour of departure, accordingly, was postponed until 10 p.m.

Evidently Lyon became so engrossed with preparations for the attack that he forgot the time. When the general left his headquarters it was midnight, 2 hours after the scheduled hour. Nevertheless, Lyon proceeded to Camp Hunter. When he reached Andrews' and Sturgis' encampment, it was 3 a.m. It was now too late to get into position in time to attack the Confederates before daybreak. The general, therefore, returned to Springfield, taking Andrews' and Sturgis' brigades with him.

On his return to Springfield, Lyon told Schofield "that he had a premonition that a night attack would prove disastrous, and yet he had felt impelled to try it once, and perhaps should do so again, 'for my only hope of success is in a surprise.' "[4]

Throughout the daylight hours on August 7, strong Confederate reconnaissance patrols operated on the southern and western approaches to Springfield. The Union cavalry was in frequent contact with these Rebels. An attack was expected at any minute. Lyon, therefore, kept his troops under arms from daybreak to dark. At frequent intervals, farmers and members of the Home Guard would come rushing into Springfield with reports that the Confederates were coming. This served to worry and exhaust the troops, thus depriving "them of the rest which was absolutely necessary to fit them for battle after their fatiguing march."

About noon, a report from some of his scouts reached Lyon indicating that a strong force of Rebel infantry, supported by two guns, was advancing on the Little York road. A force of regulars and Kansas volunteers with two of Backoff's guns was sent to engage this Confederate combat patrol. After advancing about 4½ miles, the Federals discovered that only a small Rebel mounted patrol was operating on the Little York road. These Southerners fled at the Northerners' approach. The disgusted Unionists then retraced their steps.[5]

These reports of Confederate activity had a telling effect on the civilians. Many inhabitants of Springfield became panic-stricken, hurridly packed their belongings, and departed for supposed havens of safety; others made preparations to flee the threatened city. Toward nightfall, the panic began to wane. Nevertheless, many of the people who remained did not retire or make any effort to sleep. Col. John S. Phelps' Home Guard Regiment (commanded during the colonel's absence by Col. Marcus Boyd) was on the **"qui vive** the whole night."[6]

Thursday morning (August 8) Lyon again received reports stating that the Rebels were advancing on Springfield. Lyon's army was quickly moved into battle stations, while the baggage wagons were concentrated in the center of the city. The troops were kept under arms most of the day. It was late in the afternoon before the Union officers learned that there was not any truth to the rumors telling of the foe's advance.[7]

During the afternoon, Lyon convened a council of war. At this meeting, summoned for the purpose of determining the best way to extricate the army from its precarious position, General Lyon announced to the officers:

Gentlemen, there is no prospect of our being re-enforced at this point; our supply of provisions is running short; there is a superior force in front; and it is reported that Hardee is marching with 9,000 men to cut our line of communication. It is evident that we must retreat. The question arises, what is the best method of doing it. Shall we endeavor to retreat without giving the enemy battle beforehand, and run the risk of having to fight every inch along our line of retreat, or shall we attack him in his position, and endeavor to hurt him so that he cannot follow us. I am decidedly in favor of the latter plan. I propose to march this evening with all our available force, leaving only a small guard to protect the property which will be left behind, and, marching by the . . . [Telegraph] road, throw our whole force upon him at once, and endeavor to rout him before he can recover from his surprise.[8]

Lyon's principal officers dissuaded him from carrying out this operation. They told the general, "Many of the troops were exhausted, and all were tired." In addition, a supply train had arrived from Rolla. Consequently, Lyon decided it would be best "to clothe and shoe the men as far as practicable, and to give them another day for recuperation."[9]

On the morning of August 9, a courier reached Springfield from St. Louis. The messenger carried a dispatch from Frémont addressed to Lyon. Glancing at the letter, Lyon found that Frémont did not consider his situation "critical." Frémont believed that Lyon "doubtless over-estimated the force in his front; that he ought not to fall back without good cause." Lyon was informed that no reinforcements could be sent, and "that he must report his future movements as soon as possible, and do the best he could."[10]

With Frémont's communication before him, Lyon sat down at the table in his headquarters and drafted the last letter that he ever wrote:

I have just received your note of the 6th instant by special messenger.

I retired to this place, as I have before informed you, reaching here on the 5th. The enemy followed to within 10 miles of here. He has taken a strong position, and is recruiting his supplies of horses, mules, and provisions by forages into the surrounding country, his large force of mounted men enabling him to do this without much annoyance from me. I find my position extremely embarrassing, and am at present unable to determine whether I shall be able to maintain my ground or be forced to retire. I can resist any attack from the front, but if the enemy [should] move to surround me, I must retire. I shall hold my ground as long as possible, though I may, without knowing how far, endanger the safety of my entire force, with its valuable material, being induced by the important considerations involved to take this step. The enemy yesterday made a show of force about five miles distant, and has doubtless a full purpose of making an attack upon me.[11]

After dispatching this note to Frémont, Lyon received word that one of Captain Stanley's companies of regulars and Company I, 2d Kansas Infantry (Mounted), had clashed with one of Price's mounted patrols on Grand Prairie, 5 miles west of Springfield. The Confederates fled, leaving two dead and six healthy prisoners behind. From the captives it was learned that the Southerners were suffering from a lack of provisions. To get supplies, they were compelled "to do some pretty liberal foraging on both friends and enemies."[12]

The intelligence caused Lyon to send out a reconnaissance patrol. Accordingly, the general asked Colonel Andrews to send him a company of the 1st Missouri Infantry. In response to the general's request, Company C (Capt. G. Harry Stone commanding) reported to Lyon's headquarters. Stone was told to take his men and see if there were any Confederate infantry closer to Springfield than Wilson Creek.

Accompanied by about 15 U. S. Dragoons, Stone's patrol moved out the Telegraph road about 4 miles. Here Stone halted the infantry. The captain and the troopers then advance a mile closer to the Wilson Creek encampment. Approaching a farm house, the Yankees saw several Rebels making a hurried departure. At the house, Captain Stone learned from the inhabitants that two of the recent visitors were Texans. Having obtained this information, Stone's patrol returned to Springfield, and the captain reported to General Lyon.[13]

This constituted the first definite information that the Union general had received indicating that McCulloch and Price had joined forces. Lyon decided he must act at once before the Confederates were able to consolidate their position. The general, therefore, called another meeting of his brigade, regimental, and battery commanders.

When the council of war assembled, all the principal officers except General Sweeny were present. A number of the officers insisted that the Army of the West was too small and poorly equipped to hazard a battle with the powerful Confederate host. Furthermore, it was pointed out that the superior Rebel cavalry would be able to harass the army's rear, cut its communication lines, and capture the supply trains. Frémont's message of the morning was cited as evidence that "there was but scant prospect of being reinforced before the impending battle." In addition, there was every indication that the Southerners, in overwhelming numbers, were about to descend on Springfield. The officers realized that if there were to be a fight, it must necessarily "be victory or annihilation."[14]

Lyon admitted that logic was on the side of the spokesmen urging retreat. He, however, looked at the problem from a different angle. The general reiterated his opinion that a "stubborn contest would be a better guarantee" for the column's security in case of retreat. "A bold dash, skillfully made," Lyon felt, "would astonish the foe and bewilder his judgment, even though it might not succeed in routing him." Amid the confusion of the Southerners in the wake of such a movement, the general explained, the Union soldiers would be able to retire in safety. A retreat that was conducted as proposed, with a powerful foe pressing on the rear of the Army of the West, might be the very means of its utter destruction.[15]

The general also appreciated the great calamity that would befall the people of the Union proclivities residing in southwestern Missouri if the Union army were to evacuate the area. Besides, he observed, Springfield was the place to defend St. Louis. In the event that the Federals were forced to fall back, the lines of retreat to Kansas City, Jefferson City and Rolla were still open. Finally, if Springfield were abandoned without a battle, "it might seriously damage the prestige of the national arms."[16]

Despite the logic behind Lyon's arguments, the council of war, after determining to fall back to Rolla, adjourned. Orders were issued to break camp preparatory to carrying out this movement.[17]

By this time, General Sweeny and Capt. Florence M. Cornyn (a surgeon in the 1st Missouri) had learned of the decision to give up Springfield. In separate interviews, these two officers sought successfully to get the general to change his mind. Speaking with the general on the back porch of the Boren house, Sweeny pointed out:

> . . . the disastrous results which must ensue upon a retreat without a battle — how the "rebels" would boast over such an easy conquest, how they would terrorize, harass, and persecute the unprotected Unionists if given undisputed possession of the country, how the Unionists themselves would become discouraged, crushed, or estranged.

Sweeny declared himself in favor of holding out to the last moment. He thundered, "Let us eat the last bit of mule flesh and fire the last cartridge before we think of retreating."[18]

After the volatile one-armed Irishman had departed, Lyon returned to his room and lay down on his cot. Surgeon Cornyn now called upon the general. He "was equally impressed with the impossibility of successfully retreating 120 miles before such great odds, so largely supplied with cavalry." Cornyn observed:

> The retreat would become a panic, the loss of artillery and transportation would be the smallest portion of the disaster; that the loss in men would not be near so much in a battle; and that the encouragement given to the rebellion would be in proportion to our own demoralization.[19]

Lyon now changed his mind. He would boldly seize the initiative. About this time, Colonel Sigel's chief quartermaster, Maj. Alexis Mudd, arrived at headquarters. Not knowing of the change in plans, Mudd asked Lyon, "When do we start back, General?"

Fixing his keen blue eyes on the quartermaster, Lyon replied, "When we are whipped back. Not until then."

"Yes," he continued, "that is the order. No craven shrinking from imperative duty now. Let what will come, God is eternal, and **just**."[20]

Orders were then issued alerting the officers to hold their troops ready to march at 6 p.m. Before taking the field, the soldiers were to draw all the ammunition that they could carry from the ordnance department. The troops were to move in light marching order, all unnecessary baggage would be left behind.[21]

At the staff meeting held by General Lyon on the afternoon of August 8, Colonel Sigel had proposed that his

Capt. Thomas W. Sweeny

Sweeny led the task force that marched to Forsyth, Mo., in the middle of July, to chastise Southerners occupying the town.

brigade move independently of the main column, and strike the foe on the flank and rear. This proposition was unanimously condemned by the officers present. In addition, Lyon also turned it down. When Lyon announced that he would attack the Confederates at daybreak on August 10, Sigel procured an interview with the general. This time, he succeeded in persuading Lyon "to allow him a separate command." Sigel was directed to move his command down the Yokermill road. He would then turn toward the southwest and try to gain the Confederates' flank and rear. At Sigel's request, Lyon stated that he would procure guides and cavalry to assist him. The general would also let Sigel know the exact time that his column would march. Next, Sigel asked Lyon whether, on his command's arrival near the Southerners' position, he "should attack immediately or wait until . . . [he was] appraised of the fight by the other troops." After reflecting a moment, Lyon replied, "Wait until you hear the firing on our side." The interview terminated, and Sigel returned to his quarters.[22]

While Sigel's command marched against the Confederates' rear and right, Lyon's column would move out the Little York road to a point nearly opposite the foe's advance pickets on Wilson Creek. Turning off the road, Lyon's troops would wheel sharply to the left, march across Grand Prairie, and attack the Southerners' left flank. If the plan worked, the Rebels would be caught in the jaws of a giant pincers.[23]

Shortly before sundown, the bugles were blown and the drums beaten. The various units constituting the Army of the West fell in on their colors. Since the 1st Iowa was sleeping under the stars, there were not any tents to make the regimental line. After the Iowans had been standing in line for a few minutes, General Lyon was seen approaching on his large iron-gray horse. Lyon, as he rode by, made a brief speech to each company. Pvt. Eugene F. Ware, a member of the 1st Iowa, recalled, "We could not hear what he [the general] said to the companies on each side of us, owing to the distance apart of the companies and the low tone of his voice." Reining in his horse in front of Company E, Lyon announced:

> Men, we are going to have a fight. We will march out in a short time. Don't shoot until you get orders. Fire low— don't aim higher than their knees; wait until they get close; don't get scared; it's no part of a soldier's duty to get scared.[24]

On comparing notes after Lyon had departed from the Iowans' encampment, the soldiers discovered that the gist of the general's remarks to each of the companies was the same.[25]

General Sweeny had also spoken to several of the units. Unlike Lyon, Sweeny had couched his address in terms calculated to increase the men's enthusiasm. He told the cavalry, "Stay together, boys, and we'll saber hell out of them."[26]

Shortly after Lyon's visit, the ordnance wagons were driven up and the ammunition distributed. The men of the 1st Iowa filled not only their cartridge-boxes but also the pockets in their breeches. Since the woolen shirts worn by the Iowans had pockets, most of the soldiers likewise stuffed these pockets with ammunition. A wagon from the commissary department soon appeared on the scene. The soldiers were then issued 2 days' rations of beef and pork, which they cooked immediately.[67]

Before the soldiers had finished preparing the cooked rations, a sergeant drove up in a large covered army wagon. The sergeant asked how many were "present for duty." On being answered by Sgt. Joseph Utter, he threw on the ground an equal number of "large turtle-shelled loaves" of bread. The loaves bounced in the dust, and each of the Iowans picked up one. Private Ware recalled that his:

> . . . actions regarding my loaf was perhaps descriptive of what the others did. I plugged it like a watermelon and ate my supper out of the inside. When I had finished eating I fried up a lot of beef and pork (my 2 days' rations) and crammed it into the loaf and poured in all the fat and gravy.

Next, he removed the sling from his rifled-musket, secured it to the loaf and slung it over his shoulder.[68]

IV/The Battle Opens

About 6 p.m., the adjutants shouted for the men to fall in. At a word from Lyon, the troops constituting the general's striking force moved out of their encampments located on either side of Wilson Creek at Phelps Grove. Major Sturgis' brigade took the lead as the column turned into the Little York road. Capt. Charles C. Gilbert's Company B, 1st U. S. Infantry, had the advance as the little army tramped westward. About 20 residents of the area, including Pleasant Hart and Parker Cox, were serving as guides and rode with Gilbert's vanguard.[1]

It was twilight by the time the troops reached the Grand Prairie west of Springfield. Here the road was flanked by large cornfields. The day had been hot, and with the setting of the sun it grew cooler. Private Ware recalled that "life became more endurable and the marching was anything but a funeral procession. The boys gave each other elaborate instructions as to the materials out of which they wanted their coffins made, and how they wanted them decorated."[2]

Since Lyon hoped to take the Confederates by surprise, he had given instructions for his officers to try to curb all unnecessary noise. Therefore, the cannoneers, before leaving Springfield, had wrapped the wheels of their guns, limbers, and caissons with blankets. Both the cavalry and the artillery horses had their hoofs covered with burlap

51

which was banded at the fetlock. Despite the general's instructions, the Iowa and the Kansas volunteers were disposed to exercise their vocal talents. Camp songs of all sorts were sung **con spiritu** as the troops marched along. The 1st Iowa had a favorite song, the refrain of which ran:

> So let the wide world wag as it will,
> We'll be gay and happy still.
> Gay and happy, gay and happy,
> We'll be gay and happy still.

The strains of this song carried out over Grand Prairie loud enough, it was feared, to have been heard by the Confederate outposts. Encouraged by the efforts of the Iowans, the Kansans sang, "Happy Land of Canaan," and raised the neighborhood with their efforts. Toward midnight, however, the column quieted down. Lyon was heard to remark that the Iowans "had too much levity in their composition to do good fighting." He added "that he would give them an opportunity to show what they were made of."[3]

After reaching a point about 5 miles west of the Springfield square, the head of Lyon's column left the Little York road and turned south. (The place where Lyon left the Little York road was a little east of the present-day town of Brookline.) With the guides leading the way, the Federals marched southward across Grand Prairie. At times, the troops followed unimproved byroads. The pace of the march was accordingly slowed down considerably. To make matters worse, the soldiers now left the level open prairie and moved down into the breaks which flanked Wilson Creek on the west.[4]

Private Ware recalled:

> We moved short distances from 20 to 100 yards at a time, and kept halting and closing up, and making very slow progress. Finally, we were practically involved in the timber and among the side-hills of a watercourse [Wilson Creek]. There were some little light clouds, but it was light enough to see a short distance around us, by starlight; it was in the dark of the moon. Finally, word was passed along the line that we were inside the enemy's picket, but were two or three miles from their camp. [When they were preparing to march against Lyon, the Confederates had recalled their outposts. At this hour, the Rebel picket line was unmanned.] Rumors magnified the number of the foe to 25,000. We could see the sheen in the sky of vast camp fires beyond the hills, but could not see the light. We also heard at times the choruses of braying mules.[5]

Once the Union vanguard had approached to within sight of the Confederate "guard fires," Lyon called a halt. He would wait until daybreak before resuming the advance. Accordingly, the word was passed for the men to lie down and take it easy. The main body of the Union column had halted on the Milton Norman farm about 3½ miles northeast of the unsuspecting Confederate encampment. It was about 1 a.m.[6]

Many of the troops welcomed the stop. Private Ware wrote of his experiences:

> About this time, while we were moving along we passed around the brow of a low, rocky hill, and the line stopped at a place where our company stood on a broad ledge of rock. We all laid down on this rock to get rested. The cool, dewy night air made me feel chilly in the "linings" which I was wearing; but the radiating heat which the rock during the day had absorbed, was peculiarly comfortable.[7]

General Lyon bivouacked in a cornfield near the head of the column. He shared a rubber poncho with Major Schofield. As the two officers tried to get some rest, Lyon

Maj. John M. Schofield
Adjutant to General Lyon

seemed to be "oppressed with the responsibility of his situation, with anxiety for the cause, and with sympathy for the Union people" in southwestern Missouri in case he should be forced to retreat. The general repeatedly expressed himself as having been abandoned by his superiors.[8]

While the men were resting, Lyon's scouts reconnoitered the ground over which the column would be called upon to attack.[9] They were able to penetrate to within a short distance of the Confederate camps without encountering any pickets. Having obtained the desired information, the scouts made their way back to Lyon's command post.

It was between 4 and 5 p.m. on August 9 when Sigel received instructions from General Lyon to move at 6:30 p.m. At this time, Sigel's brigade was stationed at Camp Fremont on the south side of Springfield near the Yokermill road. Sigel accordingly alerted his subordinates to hold their men ready to take the field. In the meantime, General Lyon had ordered two companies of cavalry (Company I, 1st U. S. Cavalry commanded by Capt. Eugene A. Carr and Company C, 2d Dragoons led by Lt. Charles E. Farrand) to report to Colonel Sigel at 6 p.m. Carr's and Farrand's troopers were at Sigel's command post by the designated hour. In addition to the two cavalry commands, Sigel's force consisted of eight companies of the 3d and nine companies of the 5th Missouri (912 officers and men), and six pieces of artillery manned by the cannoneers of the 1st Battery of Backoff's Missouri Light Artillery Battalion. Five guides (C. B. Owen, John Steele, Andrew Adams, Sam Carthal, and L. A. D. Crenshaw) also joined Sigel at this time.[10]

At 6:30 p.m. sharp, Sigel's brigade marched out of the encampment. Captain Carr's cavalrymen took the lead as the column marched down the Yokermill road; Lieutenant Farrand's dragoons brought up the rear. Carr's orders were to seize all persons who might carry news of the Union advance to the Confederates. After the column had traveled about 5 miles, it turned off the Yokermill road. Moving in a southwesterly direction along the old Delaware road, Sigel's troops left the prairie country and entered a wooded area. It was very dark; about 9 p.m. it started to drizzle. After a short while the rain ceased, but the sky remained overcast. It was, therefore, with considerable difficulty that the Federals found their way and kept getting separated. About 11 p.m. Sigel halted his column. So far, Captain Carr had been able successfully to discharge his assignment. No news of the Union movement had reached the foe's encampment, as Carr's troopers had arrested every person encountered, and placed guards on all the houses in the neighborhood. The troops were permitted to rest until 2 a.m., when the march was renewed.[11]

As the first streak of dawn appeared on the eastern horizon, Sigel's command resumed the march. After advancing about 1½ miles, Carr's troopers succeeded in cutting off and capturing about 40 Confederate foragers. (At the time that they were made prisoners, the Southerners were busy digging potatoes, picking roasting ears, gathering tomatoes, and procuring other supplies for their individual commissary departments.) This operation was carried out in such a fashion that none of the Rebels was able to escape and sound the alarm. On being questioned, one of the prisoners told Lieutenant Farrand "that their army was expecting re-enforcements from Louisiana, and that they had mistaken us for their re-enforcements."[12]

Shortly thereafter, Sigel, who was riding with Carr, came out on a commanding knoll. From this position, the colonel obtained an excellent view of the tents occupied by the Confederate cavalry which were located on the west side of Wilson Creek. Sigel now made his dispositions. Four of the guns manned by Backoff's battalion were manhandled into position on the hill overlooking the Rebel encampment which spread out to the Federals' front and right. Lieutenant Farrand's dragoons were called up. While the artillerists were putting their four pieces into battery, Sigel conferred briefly with Col. Charles E. Salomon. The colonel was told to take the infantry, the cavalry, and the other two guns, and ford Wilson Creek below the Rebel cantonment. Salomon's mission was to get astride the Telegraph road and cut off the Confederate avenue of retreat. A company of the 5th Missouri (K) was detached and left to guard the prisoners. As the infantrymen moved down the road leading to the ford, Carr's troopers covered their right flank and Farrand's dragoons their left.[13]

When the Union army marched out to attack the Confederates, General Lyon had left the Christian and Greene County Home Guards (about 1,200 strong) to hold Springfield. Besides garrisoning the city, the Home Guards were directed to watch the Telegraph road. In case the Federals should fail to defeat the Rebels, Springfield would have to be evacuated. Colonel Boyd of the Home Guard, therefore, made certain that everything was ready to facilitate an orderly retreat. Wagons were loaded, and the bank deposits were secured for transfer. These were closely guarded by the Home Guard.[14]

About 4 a.m., Lyon had his officers arouse their men. One of the soldiers recalled, "just as there was a slight flush of dawn in the east, somebody came along and woke us all up, and told us to keep still and fall in line." Captain Gilbert's company again had the lead as the Union column moved off. Capt. Joseph P. Plummer's regular battalion came next, followed by Major Osterhaus' Missouri battalion and Captain Totten's six-gun battery.[15]

Upon resuming the march, the Federals advanced in a southwesterly direction, with a view of striking the most northerly portion of the Confederate encampment. Except for Gilbert's soldiers who were deployed as skirmishers, Lyon's units marched in column by companies. At daylight, the Federals caught their first glimpse of the Confederate pickets. The Rebel outposts fled at the Yankees' approach. Lyon, to be on the safe side, quickly deployed Plummer's regulars into line of battle. Osterhaus' battalion was sent to the right as skirmishers, while Colonel Andrews' 1st Missouri was called up and massed in support of Totten's battery. When these dispositions were completed, the advance was renewed.[16]

Lyon's troops forged ahead rapidly. About 1½ miles were covered before the Yankee vanguard sighted any more Southerners. During this portion of the advance, the Northerners passed through a small wheat field, crossed a hill, and entered the valley where E. Ben Short's farm was located. Just as the Shorts were sitting down to breakfast, they glanced out the kitchen window and saw that their yard was full of soldiers. The men were moving on the double and the horses at the trot.[17]

As the Federal skirmishers prepared to ascend the ridge south of the Short house, they were fired upon by the Confederates (Rains' troopers). Without hesitating a moment, Captain Totten shouted for Lieutenant Sokalski to put his section into battery. Quickly unlimbering their guns, the artillerists opened fire on the Rebels ensconced on the wooded ridge to their front. Totten's other four pieces were "thrown forward into battery on the right on higher ground." Once the artillery had softened up the Rebels with a few rounds, the infantry quickly dislodged them and secured the crest of the hill. Before pressing on, Lyon halted his command to perfect his dispositions. Calling for Captain Plummer, Lyon told him to take his battalion, reinforced by Capts. Clark Wright's and Theodore A. Switzler's Home Guard Companies, and cross to the east side of Wilson Creek. Plummer's mission was to keep the Southerners from turning Lyon's left flank. Once he was in position, Plummer was to regulate the pace of his advance by that of the main column.[18]

The Union advance had taken the Confederates by surprise. During the night, the Southerners had recalled their outposts. Accordingly, the Northerners were able to penetrate very close to the Rebels' encampment without being discovered. At dawn, Colonel Cawthorn, the officer in command of Rains' mounted brigade, became apprehensive and sent a patrol up the west side of Wilson Creek. This reconnaissance patrol had not advanced more than 1½ miles beyond Gibson's Mill before the soldiers discovered that there were Yankees operating in the area. News of this important development was immediately relayed to Colonel Cawthorn. The brigade commander called for Col. De Witt C. Hunter who commanded one of his regiments. Hunter was told to take his unit (about 300 effectives) and ascertain whether the foe was advancing in force or not.

It was about 5 a.m. when Hunter's troops reached the crest of the ridge overlooking the Short farm, and sighted the head of Lyon's column. Hunter's first intention was to attack. The aggressive colonel felt that a sudden attack might throw the Union advance into confusion. By this time, however, Lyon had also spotted the Confederates. While Totten's gunners unlimbered their guns, the initial Union assault wave (Osterhaus' battalion on the right, the 1st Missouri in the center, and Plummer's battalion on the left) rolled up the hill. Confronted by this formidable force, Hunter's Confederates fell back upon their encampment.[19]

In the meantime, Colonel Cawthorn had heard the sound of the firing as the Yankees established contact with Hunter's regiment. He accordingly proceeded to dismount and form the remainder of his brigade into a line of battle on the north face of "Bloody Hill." Cawthorn (after detailing the men necessary to hold the horses) was able to deploy a total of about 600 men. When Hunter's men, falling back in the face of Lyon's push, reached Cawthorn's main line of resistance, the brigade commander halted Hunter. Cawthorn told Hunter to retire farther down the creek and dismount his men. When this business had been taken care of, Hunter would return to the front and deploy his regiment on the brigade's right flank.[20]

Upon gaining the crest of the ridge overlooking Cawthorn's camp, Lyon sighted a Confederate brigade (Cawthorn's) massed into line of battle on the opposite slope. Lyon now called up the 1st Kansas. The Kansans were ordered to take poitions on the left of the 1st Missouri. This order to move to the front reached Colonel Deitzler about 5 a.m. Before leading his Kansans into position, Deitzler rode along his regiment's line, and as one of the soldiers recalled:

> . . . electrified the spirits and hopes of his men, by utter ing a few sharp, emphatic sentences, that did more to arouse their feeling than the most elaborate speech, delivered by the most gifted and eloquent orator, could have done. Rising in his stirrups, he exclaimed in language more emphatic than reverent, "Boys, we've got them, d-m them.[21]

After the colonel had finished his speech, he led his men up the hill on the double. As they scaled the hill, the Kansans sang:

> So let the wide world wag as it will,
> We'll be gay and happy.[22]

After Hunter's mounted regiment had fallen back, Captain Totten shouted for his men to limber up their six fieldpieces. Once the artillerists had hitched up their guns, Totten led them up the ridge, hard on the heels of the infantrymen of the 1st Kansas and the 1st Missouri. Before Totten could get his guns into battery, the Kansans and Missourians had moved against Cawthorn's main line of resistance. A brief skirmish was necessary to drive the Rebels from their position. Falling back across the brow of "Bloody Hill," Cawthorn's troops took cover on its southern slope. Here, for the time being at least, they were safe. During the course of the retreat, the regiments commanded by Cols. James McCown and De Witt C. Hunter became separated from the brigade. These two units did not rejoin Cawthorn until late in the day.

The remainder of Lyon's command followed the assault wave up the ridge south of the Short farm. Crossing the head of the ravine where the now deserted tents of Cawthorn's brigade were located, the troops ascended the northern slope of "Bloody Hill." The 1st Kansas and the 1st Missouri had already crossed the crest of the hill as they pressed relentlessly after Cawthorn's defeated brigade. The Union advance, however, was suddenly slowed when a Rebel battery (Woodruff's) opened fire. From a masked position on the eastern side of Wilson Creek, the Arkansas cannoneers began to rake the attacking Yankees with shot and shell. This fire slowed the pace of the Federal's drive. Caution now became the watchword. To neutralize the effect of this shelling, Lyon directed Captain Totten to put his guns into battery. Totten accordingly placed his pieces in position on a knoll, which was a short distance west of Cawthorn's abandoned encampment. The ground occupied by the Pulaski Arkansas Battery was within easy range of Totten's guns. Captain Totten reported:

> The left half battery was then brought into position, but the right half battery, in reality occupying the most favorable ground, was principally directed against the enemy's battery, although the whole six pieces, as opportunity occurred, played upon the enemy's guns.

Since the position where Woodruff's Arkansans had emplaced their four pieces was masked from their view, the gun captains of Battery F had to use as their aiming points the flash and smoke of the opposing guns.[24]

General Rains, to whose division Cawthorn's brigade was attached, had established his headquarters on the east side of Wilson Creek near Gibson's Mill. About the time that Hunter's regiment had moved to that front, Rains had received reports from his foraging parties indicating that the Yankees were "advancing in force" on the west side of Wilson Creek and had penetrated to within 3 miles of his camp. Rains, therefore, called for Colonel Snyder, his chief of staff. Snyder was directed to go and "see what was the matter." On reaching the prairie west of the creek, he saw the Federals approaching. Hastening back to Rains, Snyder told the general that the Yankees were advancing in great force, "their soldiers and cannon covering the whole prairie." Rains ordered Snyder to carry this news to General Price.[25]

The Battle from 5 a.m. to 6 a.m.

Lyon's vanguard made contact with the Confederate pickets at dawn and pressed forward. The 1st U. S. Infantry, the 1st Missouri, and the 2d Missouri attacked Hunter's cavalry command at 5 a.m. and drove him from the ridge.

By 5 a.m., Colonel Sigel had Backoff's battery in position to shell the Southerners encamped in Sharp's Cornfield. The 3d Missouri and the 5th Missouri were poised waiting for Lyon's signal to attack.

While Hunter retreated south to Bloody Hill, Cawthorn positioned McCowan's and Peyton's cavalrymen on the north face of Bloody Hill in order to slow Lyon's advance until reinforcements arrived.

Lyon ordered Plummer and his 1st U. S. Infantry to cross Wilson Creek and guard the left flank. As Plummer moved out, the 1st Kansas took position on the left of the 1st Missouri.

The 1st Kansas and 1st Missouri composed Lyon's attacking force. These regiments crossed the ravine and charged up Bloody Hill forcing the Southerners to retreat. The rest of Lyon's column moved around the head of the hollow toward Bloody Hill.

Sigel, hearing the musket fire, ordered his battery to open fire. The Southern cavalrymen fled from Sigel's bombardment and Sigel began his advance.

The 1st Kansas and 1st Missouri reached the crest of Bloody Hill around 6 a.m. By this time Price and McCulloch were fully alerted. Price ordered his divisions up Bloody Hill to meet Lyon's attack.

As the 1st Kansas and 1st Missouri continued to press forward, they were shelled and thus slowed down by the Pulaski Arkansas Battery. Totten's battery opened fire on Pulaski Battery in an effort to silence the Confederate cannon.

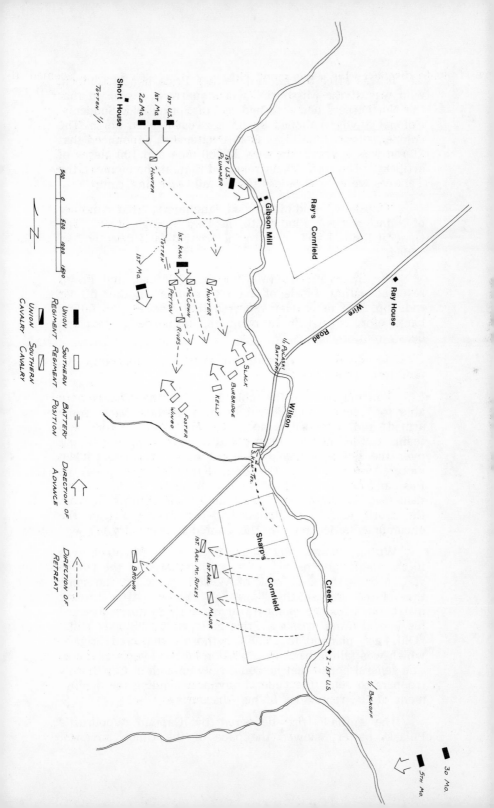

Short House
Totten ≡
1st U.S.
1st Mo.
2d Mo.
Hunter

1st U.S. Plummer
Gibson Mill
Rays Cornfield

1st Kan.
Totten ≡
1st Mo.
McCown
Peyton
Hunter
Hunter
Rives
Slack
Burbridge
Kelly
Winco
Foster

Pulaski Battery
Wire Road
Ray House

Wilson
Skegg's Tr.
Sharp's
Cornfield
Brown
1st Ark. Mt. Rifles
1st Ark.
Major
Creek
1-1st U.S.
Backoff

3d Mo.
5th Mo.

N

500   0   500   1000   1500

Union Regiment

Southern Regiment

Battery Position

Union Cavalry

Southern Cavalry

Direction of Advance

Direction of Retreat

It was after 5 a.m. and neither Price nor McCulloch, who was at the Missourian's headquarters, suspected that the Northerners had marched out of Springfield. Suddenly, Colonel Snyder galloped up on a sweat-flecked horse. The colonel, almost breathless from excitement, announced that "Lyon was approaching with 20,000 men and 100 pieces of artillery." The staff officer reported that, at the moment, the Yankees were "within less than a mile of Rains' camp."[26]

"O, pshaw," said McCulloch, laughingly, "that's another of Rains' scares," alluding to the Dug Springs affair. "Tell General Rains I will come to the front myself directly," he added.[27]

The three officers (McCulloch, McIntosh, and Price) resumed eating. Inside of 2 or 3 minutes, another officer rode up. The newcomer reported that "Rains was falling back before overwhelming numbers, and needed instant and heavy reinforcements."[28]

McCulloch again expressed disbelief, remarking, "O, nonsense! That's not true."[29]

Glancing up from the table, however, the officers were able to "see a great crowd of men on horseback, some armed, and others unarmed, mixed in with wagons and teams and led horses, all in dreadful confusion, scampering over the hill and rushing toward us — a panic-stricken mob." Moments later, the Confederate officers "saw the flash and heard the report" of Totten's guns. Then, in quick response, the sound of Sigel's guns came drifting in from the south. (Sigel's artillerists had just opened fire on the encampments occupied by the Confederate cavalry.)[30]

Within seconds, McCulloch, followed by McIntosh, was in the saddle and on his way to take charge of the troops stationed on the east bank of Wilson Creek. At the same time, Price ordered the "long roll" beaten. After leaving instructions for the members of his staff to hurry forward his infantry and artillery, Price galloped up "Bloody Hill." "Old Pap" planned to rally Cawthorn's shattered brigade which was falling back in confusion before Lyon's advance. The general hoped that he could rally enough of Cawthorn's troopers to delay the Federal advance, pending the deployment of the remainder of his Missourians.[31]

The enfilade fire delivered by Captain Woodruff's Pulaski battery slowed the pace of the Union advance.

Therefore, Price was able to regroup a portion of Cawthorn's brigade. "Old Pap" re-formed the dismounted cavalrymen several hundred yards south of the crest of "Bloody Hill." Here, the shaken troopers were screened by the dense undergrowth. Better still, they were in defilade and no longer exposed to the fire of Totten's battery.[32]

Upon being alerted that the Unionists had attacked Cawthorn's brigade, General Slack quickly mustered his two infantry units — Col. John T. Hughes' regiment and Maj. John C. C. Thornton's battalion. Slack had Colonel Hughes form the two organizations into line of battle. When these dispositions were completed, Hughes led the cheering troops (650 strong) up the southeastern face of "Bloody Hill." As they moved forward on the double, Slack's Missourians observed that the Yankees were already in possession of the crest of the hill. In accordance with Slack's directions, Hughes put the infantrymen into position on the left of Cawthorn's badly mauled command. As Slack's soldiers ascended the hill, they encountered "a most terrific fire of cannon shot and volleys of small-arms." Some confusion ensued. Slack's Missourians, in spite of this galling fire, quickly dressed their ranks, and began to blaze away at the foe.[33]

Brig. Gen. William Y. Slack
Commanded a brigade of the Missouri State Guard

General Clark was at breakfast when one of General Price's aides, Col. Richard Gaines, rode up to his headquarters. Without bothering to salute, Gaines told Clark "that the enemy were upon us." The staff officer told Clark that Price wanted him to form his command on "Bloody Hill." Clark was to post his Third Division of the Missouri State Guard alongside any other units which might have reached the hill ahead of his command. Since his cavalry battalion commanded by Colonel Major was camped in the valley south of Skegg's Branch, Clark sent one of his staff officers (Lt. Col. Richard H. Musser) to recall the troopers. Clark shouted instructions for Col. John Q. Burbridge to form his infantry regiment. Before many minutes had elapsed, Burbridge had mustered his soldiers. The general then led Burbridge's infantrymen toward the point of danger. Capt. Joseph Finks, a staff officer, was left behind with instructions to order Colonel Major to follow with his command. (Sigel's attack on the Confederate cavalry's encampment kept Major's battalion pinned down. Major, therefore, was unable to move to Clark's assistance as directed.)[34]

Before Clark had moved more than 300 yards from his encampment, he discovered that the foe was strongly on . . . [his] front upon the heights." At this time, the Yankees were already locked in a desperate contest with Slack's division. Clark quickly formed Burbridge's regiment on Slack's left.[35]

At an early hour on the morning of August 10, General Parsons received a message from General Price telling of the Union attack on Cawthorn's brigade. In addition, Parsons was directed to move to Cawthorn's assistance "with all possible dispatch with . . . [his] whole force." Parsons hurridly mustered his division. The four-gun battery commanded by Capt. Henry Guibor was put in motion first. Parsons' one infantry regiment (led by Col. Joseph M. Kelly) closely followed the artillerists. Of necessity, Parsons' line of march passed through an area covered by a dense growth of underbrush. After advancing about ½-mile, Parsons reached an open space which was suitable for the emplacement of his artillery. Orders were immediately issued for Captain Guibor to place his four guns in battery. Unlimbering their pieces, the Missourians opened fire on a strong force of Yankees (probably Colonel Andrews' regiment) which had closed to within "musket-range" of Parsons' front. Colonel Kelly's regiment was posted on the left of Guibor's guns, its right flank resting on Burbridge's left.[36]

When the alarm was sounded, General Parsons sent one of his aides (Colonel Good) to order up Colonel Brown's cavalry regiment. Brown's command, along with most of the other cavalry units attached to McCulloch's army, was bivouacked between Skegg's Branch and Terrell Creek. (Before Good was able to contact Brown, Sigel had attacked the cantonment occupied by the Rebel cavalry west of Wilson Creek.)[37]

Like General Clark, General McBride was at breakfast when the alarm sounded. Before McBride was able to form his two infantry regiments, Sigel's guns had growled into action. Despite this distraction, McBride completed his dispositions. His soldiers, upon moving out of their encampment, "marched toward the high ground to the northwest." Drawing abreast of Price's main line of resistance, McBride deployed his division on the left of Captain Guibor's battery. At this stage of the conflict, McBride's soldiers held the left flank of Price's battle line.[38]

About sunrise, Captain Croucher (the regimental drill-master) in Col. Ben Rives' unit rode excitedly into camp and informed the colonel "that the enemy was approaching and was within less than 400 yards." (Colonel Rives' cavalry regiment of Slack's division was camped near the head of the ravine which scarred the south face of "Bloody Hill.") Rives immediately ordered out 20 mounted scouts to check on this report. Simultaneously, the colonel shouted for the wagoners to hitch up their teams and for every sixth man to lead off the "led horses." Before the wagons could be removed or the men formed into battleline, the Yankees popped over the crest of "Bloody Hill" about 300 yards east of Rives' camp. The Federals immediately opened fire. While the Union infantry raked the Rebels with well-aimed volleys, Totten's gunners hammered them with shell and canister. Lt. Col. A. J. Austin and two privates were cut down by this fire. Rives accordingly shouted for his regiment to fall back. When retiring, Rives' command divided. The colonel, with about 70 dismounted troopers, fell in with Slack's infantry as it moved to the front. Various other companies from Rives' regiment attached themselves to the first command which presented itself.[39]

Weightman's infantry brigade of Rains' division had camped on the east side of Wilson Creek at Manley's Spring. While the soldiers were busy preparing breakfast, the sound of firing came drifting in from the northwest (Totten's guns firing on Hunter's combat patrol). Shortly thereafter, the troops were startled when the roar of cannons came rolling up from the southwest. (Sigel had launched his attack on the encampment of the Confederate cavalry.) Without a moment's hesitation, Weightman turned his command out under arms.

The colonel eagerly awaited his marching orders, which were not long in arriving. An aide came galloping up and directed Weightman to move to Price's assistance. At a word from Weightman, the brigade moved off in a north-westerly direction. Reaching the plateau near the Guinn house, Weightman called for Maj. Ezra H. Brashear of the 2d Regiment. Brashear was directed to take his command and post it in support of the Pulaski battery. In the next breath, Weightman told Col. Thomas H. Rosser to take his command (the 1st Regiment and the 4th Battalion) and Captain Bledsoe's battery and hasten to the cavalry's assistance. After fording Wilson Creek, Rosser led his men down the Telegraph road toward the Sharp house.

Accompanied by the 3d and 5th regiments (about 700 strong), Weightman crossed Wilson Creek at the ford. Pushing up the southeastern face of "Bloody Hill," he used his two regiments to plug the gap that had opened between Slack's division and Cawthorn's brigade. Weightman's hardy soldiers reached the field about ½-hour after McBride's troopers had moved into position on Parsons' left.[40]

The main line of resistance which Price succeeded in organizing to dispute Lyon's advance, following the arrival of Weightman's two regiments, was held by over 3,100 men and four cannons. Furthermore, Price's Missourians received considerable assistance from the four guns of the Pulaski Arkansas Battery emplaced on the east side of the creek. From their position at the Guinn house, the Arkansas cannoneers were able to enfilade the Union line of advance.[41]

In the meantime, Sigel's column had launched its attack on the encampment occupied by the Confederate cavalry. About 5:30 a.m. Sigel distinctly heard the sound of musketry from the northwest. This announced to Sigel the approach of Lyon. He, therefore, ordered the four guns emplaced on the commanding ridge opposite the mouth of Terrell Creek to open fire. The gunners of Backoff's battalion had previously sighted their four guns. When Sigel gave the word,

Lts. G. A. Schaeffer and Edward Schuetzenbach barked out the command "Fire!"

"Boom! Boom! Boom! Boom!," in rapid succession, went the four fieldpieces as the gun captains pulled the lanyards. Sigel recalled that the early morning bombardment "had a 'stirring' effect on the enemy." Quickly reloading their pieces, the Union artillerists sent several more rounds crashing into the camp.[42]

While the shelling threw the Rebel encampment into the wildest confusion, it failed to inflict many casualties. One of the Union officers recalled:

> . . . our guns being on an elevation, and the Confederates being in a field which sloped toward the creek, the shots passed over their heads, creating a stampede but doing little, if any damage to life or limb. In vain I and others urged the artilleryment to depress the guns. Either from inability to understand English, or, in the excitement, thinking it was only necessary to load and fire, they kept banging away till the whole camp was deserted.[43]

To cover the march of Salomon's infantry as it moved down to the ford, Captain Carr's troopers dismounted and took position near the edge of the bluff overlooking the Southerners' cantonment. When the guns roared into action, Carr's men discharged several volleys into the milling Confederates. Since the range was near the maximum for his men's carbines, Carr's only purpose for carrying out this operation was to distract the Rebels.[44]

Sigel's attack took the cavalrymen of General Steen's loosely organized Third Division by surprise. Only a few minutes before, Colonel Musser had handed Colonel Major his instructions to move to General Clark's assistance. When Sigel's artillery and Carr's cavalry suddenly opened fire, Major's troopers were busy saddling their mounts. Many of the men's horses were unused to cannon fire and stampeded. Unable to form his command while it was being shelled, Major shouted for his men to take to the woods. Here, the colonel succeeded in rallying his battalion. Major then tried to join Clark. As Major's troopers endeavored to beat their way through the woods, mounted men from other commands dashed madly through their ranks. Confusion prevailed. When Major reached the Telegraph road, he discovered that all his battalion with the exception of one company had straggled.[45]

Sigel's sudden attack took completely by surprise Colonel Brown's regiment and its three attached companies. Nevertheless, Brown made a "gallant and desperate attempt to form his men in the field under this murderous fire." Brown, however, failed. The troopers retired into the timber west of the Telegraph road. Here the colonel rallied his command. Next, the cavalrymen moved northward in an effort to rejoin Parsons' division. Before he reached Skegg's Branch, Brown encountered General McCulloch. The general ordered the colonel to turn his unit around and cooperate with Colonel Greer's command.[46]

About sunrise, Colonel Greer had received instructions from McCulloch's headquarters to report with his regiment at the ford where the Telegraph road crossed Wilson Creek. The staff officer who delivered this message to Greer told him that the Yankees "had fired upon some of our soldiers." At this time, the Texans had already saddled their horses. Hardly had the aide delivered this dispatch before Sigel's guns opened fire on the cavalry's encampment. Once the regiment had been formed, Greer determined to cross Wilson Creek at the ford opposite General Pearce's camp and assail Sigel's artillery. When Greer gave the order, the head of the column moved off. Before the colonel had proceeded very far, he discovered that about one-half of his regiment had failed to get the word. These companies, instead of fording the creek, had remained in camp. Greer accordingly sent his adjutant racing to the rear with instructions for the missing units to rejoin the regiment.[47]

By this time, Sigel's troops had forded Terrell Creek. Guns had been placed in battery and the cannoneers of Backoff's battalion were again hammering away at the Confederate encampment. Maj. George W. Chilton (as the senior officer present) had assumed charge of the battalion of Greer's regiment that had failed to cross the creek. Spotting the Union battleline, Chilton quickly formed his battalion into line of battle. Greer, upon observing this situation, reversed his line of march. When he endeavored to recross the creek, he found the ford choked with wagons. While Greer's Texans were trying to clear the road and pass around the stalled wagons, Capt. William R. Bradfute (one of McCulloch's aides) rode up. The captain told Greer "that the main body of the enemy was up the creek on the west side of the stream on a large hill ["Bloody Hill"]." Greer, for the time being, decided to forego uniting his regiment.

He, therefore, led the battalion which had accompanied him up Skegg's Branch.[48]

The troopers of the 1st Arkansas Mounted Rifles were preparing breakfast when Sigel's guns started to shell their camp. Since his men were bivouacked in an open field and exposed to a raking fire and lacked any artillery support, Colonel Churchill shouted for them to take cover in the woods. Taking advantage of the protection afforded by the trees, Churchill succeeded in forming his regiment. He then led his regiment northeastward along the Telegraph road.[49]

Colonel Carroll's 1st Arkansas Cavalry was also routed from its camp by the fire of Sigel's artillery. Once his men had reached the woods, Colonel Carroll succeeded in rallying his badly shaken regiment. Like Churchill, Carroll then led his regiment up the Telegraph road. When he reached Skegg's Branch, Carroll was ordered up the hollow.[50]

In the meantime, Sigel's column had waded Wilson Creek. As the Yankees pressed ahead, Lieutenant Farrand's dragoons sighted a small Confederate patrol. In an effort to keep the Southerners from spreading the alarm, Farrand, followed by several of his men, raced ahead. The Rebels, however, sighted the oncoming Yankees. Securing their horses, the scouts rode off at a fast pace. In spite of their being unable to overtake the Southerners, Farrand's dragoons did succeed in cutting them off from their camp, "which was now in plain sight."[51]

When Sigel was informed of this episode, he decided to attack the camp. He rejoined the infantry column and had the soldiers throw down the rail fences at Dixon's farm. His troops then crossed Dixon's field and forded Terrell Creek. Riding out of the bottom of the creek, Sigel observed that he had emerged into a valley which extended northward about ¾-mile to the Sharp house. From east to west, the valley was about ½-mile across. Advancing, the Federal infantry and artillery marched along the road which bounded on the west the large field where the Rebel cavalry had pitched their tents. Flanking the road on the east was a fence; on the west was a thick woods.[52]

By the time Sigel's column had covered half the distance between Terrell Creek and the Sharp house, the colonel observed that a strong force of Rebel cavalry had taken position in the valley, not far from its northern extremity. Sigel estimated this Confederate force to number "about 3,000 strong." (Actually, only Major Chilton's battalion of the South Kansas-Texas Regiment, reinforced by scattered units from the other cavalry commands, was deployed to contest Sigel's sweep up the valley of Wilson Creek. At the most, this Confederate force could not number more than 1,000 officers and men.) The colonel accordingly halted his troops on the road. A staff officer was sent galloping to the rear, to order up the four guns that had been left on the east side of Wilson Creek. As soon as Sigel learned that these guns were approaching, he directed the head of the column to turn to the right.

Once the infantry had moved into the field east of the wood, Sigel had his two regimental commanders deploy their soldiers into line of battle — the 3d Missouri was formed on the right, the 5th Missouri on the left. The six guns of Backoff's battalion were placed in battery on the left of the infantry. Lieutenant Farrand's dragoons covered the left flank of Sigel's battleline. When his dispositions were completed, Sigel directed the artillerists to open fire. After undergoing a bombardment of about ½-hour's duration, the Confederate horsemen "retired in some confusion into the woods and up the adjoining hills."

Captain Carr, who arrived on the scene after the Southerners had retreated, reported, "the cavalry had formed to charge, and had been broken up by Colonel Sigel and put to flight, though their officers raved and stormed and tore their hair in trying to make their men advance."[53]

At this time, Captain Carr's troopers were operating on the bluff east of Wilson Creek. From his vantage point, he was able to see the Rebel cavalrymen scatter to the winds as they fled to escape the fire of Sigel's four guns. Wagons and horsemen could be observed moving off toward the west and down to Telegraph road toward Terrell Creek. Suddenly, Carr spotted the force which Major Chilton had assembled to oppose Sigel's sweep. After sending a messenger racing ahead to alert Sigel to this danger, Carr moved to rejoin the column. His troopers had to back track to the ford to get across Wilson Creek. Consequently, Sigel had already dealt with the Texans by the time Carr's troopers rode up.[54]

Following the Confederates' retreat, Lieutenant Farrand rode through their deserted encampment. The lieutenant reported that he:

. . . saw many dead bodies and quantities of arms and all descriptions lying on the ground. Many of the latter . . . [he] caused [his] men to destroy. There were in this camp a wagon load of Maynard rifles, one of regular rifled muskets, and several boxes of United States regulation sabers, all new.[55]

In the lull that followed the Southerners' retreat, Sigel observed that the sound of the firing from the northwest had increased in tempo and had drawn nearer. It was evident to Sigel that Lyon "had engaged the enemy along the whole line." To afford the greatest possible assistance to Lyon, Sigel determined to resume the advance. He planned to attack the Rebel battleline that was opposing Lyon in the rear.[56]

Sigel issued orders for his subordinates to reassemble their units on the road which flanked the fields on the west. Captain Carr was directed to cover Sigel's left flank. The march was then resumed. Pushing ahead, the Federal made their "way through a large number of cattle and horses." Several hundred yards southwest of the Sharp house, Sigel's column struck the Telegraph road. A short distance beyond was a knoll, which had been used as a slaughter yard by the Confederates. This eminence was adjacent to the Sharp house, and would provide a commanding position for Sigel's artillery.[57]

At Sharp's farm, Sigel's troops bagged a number of Confederate prisoners. These "summer soldiers and sunshine patriots" came straggling to the rear to escape the fighting that was raging on "Bloody Hill" and in the cornfield east of Wilson Creek. Evidently, these slackers were unaware that Sigel's men had blocked the Telegraph road. In all, his brigade captured about 100 Southerners. Sigel, after a brief conference with some of his officers, concluded that Lyon had been successful and was driving the Rebels before him. Realizing that the Telegraph road was the only practicable line of retreat for the Southerners and imagining that here was a "grand opportunity for stopping it up and bagging several thousand 'rebels,'" Sigel quickly deployed his men across the road. The 3d Missouri was posted on the right, the 5th Missouri on the left; four guns of Backoff's battalion were unlimbered on the plateau, the two other field pieces were held in reserve; Carr's troopers watched the area to the left of the road block; Farrand's dragoons covered the ground between the right of the brigade and Wilson Creek.[58]

71

Col. Franz Sigel
Commanded the Second Brigade at Wilson's Creek

Once he had deployed his command on the plateau, Sigel had the cannoneers open a harassing fire on the rear of one of Price's units (Burbridge's regiment) which was fighting its way up "Bloody Hill." Sigel's gunners also attacked Colonel Rosser's command. (Rosser, on learning of Sigel's rapid approach, had deployed his command [the 1st regiment and 4th battalion of Weightman's brigade and Bledsoe's battery] on the southern slope of "Bloody Hill." Rosser's mission was to keep Sigel from attacking Price's rear.) This bombardment lasted about 30 minutes.[59]

Suddenly, the firing on the part of the Confederates practically died out. Sigel, fearful lest he fire on Lyon's troops, ordered his gunners out of action. At this time (it was about 8:30 a.m.), there was a complete hiatus in military operations on the north side of Skegg's Branch. Not a shot was heard. Through the smoke of battle, Sigel was able to observe a large number of Confederates moving southward along a ridge about 700 yards away and opposite his right flank. He theorized that these Southerners were fleeing from Lyon's victorious legions.[60]

While Sigel's command was taking position, some of his men visited the captured Confederate encampment. Dr. Samuel H. Melcher (an assistant surgeon assigned to the 5th Missouri), accompanied by his orderly, visited a camp abandoned by one of the Arkansas units. There, the doctor "found a good breakfast of coffee, biscuit and fried green corn."

Shortly after the doctor rejoined his command, a number of stragglers from the 3d and 5th Missouri set fire to some of the abandoned wagons and camp equipage.[61]

V/Cornfield Fight and Rout of Sigel's Column

When McCulloch left Price's headquarters at the beginning of Lyon's attack, he crossed to the east side of Wilson Creek. Colonel McIntosh accompanied the general. Before the general had reached his command post, the fire of Sigel's artillery had thrown the camps of the Confederate cavalry into confusion. McCulloch's first objective was to dispose of the troops stationed on the left bank of the creek in a fashion calculated to cope with Sigel's advance. At this time, McCulloch had no way of knowing either the strength or purpose of Sigel's thrust.[1]

Calling for Capt. Charles A. Carroll, McCulloch told the captain to alert General Pearce. Riding up to Pearce's headquarters, Carroll found Pearce's troops already forming. Only moments before, Sergeant Hite of Pearce's bodyguard had dashed up to the general's tent, "breathless with excitement, hatless, and his horse covered with foam." The sergeant had exclaimed, "General, the enemy is coming!"

"Where?," inquired Pearce.

Hite, pointing toward the east in the direction of a spring where he had gone for water, hurriedly announced that he had been shot at by a Union patrol. Hite was ordered to carry this information to McCulloch. Pearce ordered the "long roll" beaten and the camp called to arms. When this business was taken care of, he proceeded to place his command in position to receive the Union attack. Since he and Colonel Weightman had thoroughly reconnoitered the area on the previous day, Pearce was familiar with the area. He, therefore, knew in advance where he wanted his unit commanders to deploy their men.[2]

NOTE TO THE MAP.

The engagement began at 5:30 A. M., Lyon's [ad]vance driving Rains over Bloody Hill. Price's li[ne] as formed to confront the main attack by Ly[on] about 6:30 was, from left to right, as follows: [Mc]Bride, Parsons (with Guibor's battery), Clark, Sla[ck,] and Rains. This force numbered 3168 men wit[h] guns, and was opposed by nearly 2000 men wit[h] guns. The right of the first Union line was held [by] the 1st Missouri; on its left were Totten's batte[ry,] Osterhaus's battalion, the 1st Kansas, DuBois's b[at]tery, and Steele's battalion. Later, the 1st Kan[sas] was relieved by the 1st Iowa (800), and the 1st M[is]souri by the 2d Kansas (600), and by Steele. T[his] brought the Union strength at this point up to 3[?]. Meanwhile, Hébert's 3d Louisiana and McIntos[h's] regiment and McRae's battalion, together nu[m]bering 1320, moved down from their encampme[nt] (marked "McCulloch's [bri]gade"), crossed the ro[ad,] and repulsed Plummer's [?] in the corn-field, but we[re] driven back by DuBois's b[at]tery. By this hour (8 o'clo[ck]) Sigel had attacked on t[he] rear and had driven Chur[ch]ill's infantry and Gree[ne] and Major's cavalry out [of] their camps. McCullo[ch] now gathered up part [of] the 3d Louisiana and rout[ed] Sigel's troops, who were [at] Sharp's farm. He was aid[ed] in this by the fire of Rei[d] and Bledsoe's batteri[es.] Woodruff's battery b[een] from the start chiefly [en]gaged Totten; and n[ext] Churchill, and next Gree[ne] and Carroll's cavalry, a[nd] afterward Gratiot's re[gi]ment (of Pearce's briga[de]) were conducted to the a[id] of Price, raising his for[ce] to 4239, exclusive of Gre[ene] and Carroll, who had be[en] quickly repulsed by Totte[n;] Lyon's being as abo[ve] 3550, exclusive of 220 [of] Plummer's and 350 of t[he] Mounted Reserve. Gener[al] Lyon was killed at 10:[30,] just as Pearce's fresh re[gi]ments (under Walker a[nd] Dockery) and the 3d Lo[ui]siana were coming up. [At] 11:30 Major Sturgis wit[h]drew the Union army, whi[ch] was then outnumbered tw[o] to one.

EDITORS.

BATTLE OF
WILSON'S CREEK
OR
OAK HILLS.
AUGUST 10TH 1861.

UNION   CONFEDERATE

The four guns of Captain Reid's Fort Smith Arkansas Battery were unlimbered on the edge of the plateau overlooking the mouth of Skegg's Branch. Col. J. D. Walker's 4th Arkansas Infantry was posted in support of Reid's smoothbores. (Since Colonel Walker was ill, the division adjutant, Col. Frank A. Rector, commanded the regiment in the ensuing battle.) Pearce deployed the 3rd and 5th Arkansas Infantry on the right of the 4th Arkansas. Captain Carroll's company of cavalry was held in reserve and took position in Manley Hollow. The three Arkansas infantry regiments, reinforced by the Fort Smith Battery, held the bluff overlooking the east bank of Wilson Creek from a point opposite the mouth of Skegg's Branch to the ford. These dispositions enabled Pearce to command the crossing of Skegg's Branch over which Sigel would have to pass if he planned to take Price's Missourians in the rear.[3]

In the meantime, McCulloch formed the regiments of his brigade (the 2d Arkansas Mounted Rifles, the 3d Arkansas Infantry Battalion, and the 3d Louisiana Infantry) on the plateau on the left of Pearce's right flank regiment, the 3d Arkansas. Captain Woodruff's four-gun Pulaski Arkansas Battery took position on the knoll near the Guinn house.[4]

Before McCulloch had completed his dispositions, Captain Woodruff observed that a portion of Lyon's column (Plummer's battalion) had forded Wilson Creek. At this moment, Woodruff reported, the Federals were moving toward his battery. This intelligence caused McCulloch to alter his dispositions. Colonel Gratiot's 3d Arkansas Infantry was shifted to the right and posted in support of Woodruff's guns. McIntosh — with his regiment (the 2d Arkansas Mounted Rifles), the 3d Arkansas Infantry Battalion, and the 3d Louisiana Infantry — was given the task of engaging the oncoming Unionists.[5]

McIntosh quickly assembled his striking force. Since the supervision of this force would occupy his full attention, he placed the next ranking officer (Lt. Col. Benjamin T. Embry) in temporary charge of his regiment — the 2d Arkansas Mounted Rifles. Already the Union artillery (Du Bois' battery) had started to shell the Confederate troops on the east side of the creek. To shelter his troopers from the fire of the Union guns, Colonel Embry had them take cover in the timber north of Woodruff's guns. Here, the colonel dismounted his command. McIntosh now appeared. At a word from him, the 3d Louisiana, closely followed by the 2d Arkansas Mounted Rifles, took up the advance. The 3d Arkansas Battalion, which had formed on the left of the Louisiana regiment, remained behind when McIntosh's task force took up the advance.

After following the Telegraph road for a short distance, McIntosh turned off onto a "narrow by-road flanked on both sides by the thickest kind of underbrush and on one side by a rail fence." Though covered by the fire of the Pulaski battery, McIntosh's soldiers were harassed by the fire of Du Bois' guns, which hurled canister and shell at them from the eastern brow of "Bloody Hill." Reaching a large cornfield, Colonel Hébert started to deploy his Louisianians from column into line of battle. Only two companies had been formed when the Yankees, who were lying in wait behind a rail fence, sent a volley crashing into Hébert's regiment. In the face of this galling fire, Hébert deployed the remainder of his regiment in the brush which bounded the field on the south. Colonel Embry's regiment now appeared on the scene and took position on the left of the Louisianians.[6]

Shortly after the 3d Louisiana started forward, Colonel McRae was directed by General McCulloch to countermarch his battalion. McRae was to cross Wilson Creek and take position on the crest of the hill west of the Sharp house. The colonel immediately moved out at the head of his battalion. Before the Arkansans started up the hill leading to the Sharp house, a mounted column broke through their ranks. In the confusion that followed, the battalion broke in two. Only the lead company and several files of the second remained with McRae. (The rest of the battalion, becoming separated from McRae, failed to cross Skegg's Branch. The company commanders halted their men and waited for news of the whereabouts of the colonel and the rest of the battalion.) With this force, McRae proceeded to the summit of the hill. He then deployed his men as skirmishers and posted them along the crest of the ridge, several hundred yards west of the Telegraph road. At this time, many small disorganized knots of Rebel cavalrymen were wandering willy-nilly about the area.[7]

About the only organized mounted force present was Colonel Major's greatly reduced battalion. Major used his troopers to support McRae's infantry. Before Sigel's appearance, Major's Missourians crossed to the north side of Skegg's Branch.[8]

Several minutes after McRae had formed his command, the Arkansans were startled when a battery (Backoff's) roared into action a short distance east of their position. The thick brush prevented Colonel McRae from catching a glimpse of the guns. He therefore halted several of the mounted stragglers who were hovering in the area. These men were sent to see whether friend or foe manned the guns. The troopers soon returned with the news that the battery was served by Rebels. Unsatisfied with this report, McRae sent several other cavalrymen to check on the guns. Returning, they invariably told McRae that the battery belonged to Weightman's brigade. McRae, however, taking cognizance of the direction of the firing, strongly suspected that the unseen battery was Federal. Finally, he sent two of his men to reconnoiter the guns. The two infantrymen returned and correctly identified the guns as Yankee. McRae, without a moment's hesitation, directed his men to charge "at trail arms."[9]

As soon as the Federals were sighted advancing across the north face of "Bloody Hill," the Pulaski battery roared into action. Since the fire of this battery enfiladed Lyon's advance, it was most effective. Some time before the engagement, Captain Woodruff had assigned an officer to each piece. The officers were to assist and relieve the gunners. Woodruff took his battle station at Gun Number 2. His piece fired the first shot; the others followed in rapid succession.[10]

At first, Totten's guns returned the Pulaski battery's fire. Later, Totten's cannoneers shifted targets and Du Bois' battery dueled with Woodruff's guns. Within the first hour, Lt. Omer P. Weaver was cut down by a solid shot, which broke his right arm and crushed his chest. (The young lieutenant had just been relieved by his gunner, Sgt. William D. Blocker.) Woodruff was informed that Weaver wanted to see him. Leaving his gun, Woodruff hastened to the fallen lieutenant's side. Weaver, who was lying on the ground with his shattered arm resting on his chest, told Woodruff, "I am done for; can't you have me moved?"

The captain replied, "Yes, immediately, and I will try and get a surgeon."

Weaver bravely answered, "All right; you had better go back to your gun or post."

Retracing his steps, Woodruff called for Sgt. Charles E. Button and told him to detail men to move Weaver. In addition, the sergeant was to see if he could find a surgeon.

All this time, the battery and counter-battery fire continued. Pvt. Hugh K. Byler was hit by a solid projectile above the knee; Pvt. Richard Byrd was struck in the leg by a minie ball. Both of these men were evacuated.

Sergeant Button finally managed to locate Doctor Dunlap. The doctor sought to comfort the wounded men. During the bombardment, the battery also lost two horses.[11]

In the meantime, Lyon's initial assault wave (the 1st Kansas and the 1st Missouri) had driven across the crest of "Bloody Hill." The Federals now endeavored to force their way down the south slope. General Price, by this time, had succeeded in forming his main line of resistance. The Federals had lost the advantage that the element of surprise had previously given them.

At this time, the "bang" of a cannon was heard drifting up from the south. It came from the direction where Sigel was supposed to be operating. Sturgis mistakenly thought he heard an answering report. He calculated the supposed line of fire of these two batteries as being apparently east to west and approximately at right angles to Totten's. After about 10 or 12 shots, this firing abruptly ceased. Nothing more was heard of Sigel's brigade until about 7 a.m., when a brisk cannonading was distinctly audible for a few minutes. Sturgis placed this firing about a mile to the right of that previously heard and farther away.[12]

Lyon's battleline now pressed forward. The firing, which had been spirited for the past half hour, now increased to a continuous roar, heard in Springfield. For the better part of the next 30 minutes, the battle waxed hot and heavy.[13]

At first, the battlelines were not more than 300 yards apart. Except in a few isolated instances, the combatants were concealed from one another by the intervening foliage. Since Price's Missourians were armed almost exclusively with shotguns and common rifles, it was mandatory for the general (since the opposing forces were so near to each other) either to close with Lyon's battleline, or wait for the Federals to assail his position. Price chose the latter alternative — he would let the Yankees attack.

Price did not have to wait long. In a few minutes, the command "Forward!" was distinctly heard. It was followed by the tramp of men and the crackling of brush. When Lyon's soldiers closed to within easy range of Price's Missourians, "there rang upon the air the sharp click of a 1,000 rifles and the report of a 1,000 shotguns." Missourian and Kansan now fought to the death against Missourian on the leafy hillside, while, from the opposing heights, Totten (who had been stationed at Little Rock where his family still resided) fought furiously against Woodruff.[14]

When Guibor's battery started to rake his advance, Colonel Andrews shouted for the men of the 1st Missouri to get ready to charge the guns. Before the colonel could complete his dispositions, he observed that a strong force of Rebels (McBride's division) were about to try to turn his right flank. Andrews accordingly decided to abandon his attempt to capture the artillery. Simultaneously, the colonel sent a messenger to point out the location of the Rebel battery to Captain Totten. To cope with this threat to his right flank, Andrews posted part of his regiment at right angles to his line of battle. Opening fire, these men succeeded in throwing back McBride's soldiers.

Guibor's battery had continued to play on Andrews' regiment. To make matters worse, the soldiers made a startling discovery when they picked up several unexploded shells. Examining these projectiles, the infantrymen pronounced them to be the same as those supplied to Sigel's column. (There was no truth to this conjecture. The Union soldiers, however, did not know this.) Therefore, the rumor caused considerable uneasiness when it spread through the ranks.

All this time, the left wing of Andrews' regiment had been trading volleys with Parsons' and Clark's troops. Satisfied that the right wing would be able to hold its own, Colonel Andrews rode toward the left. As he passed each company, the colonel "found it well up to its work, both officers and men cool and determined, using their arms with care and precision."[15]

79

The 1st Kansas held the ground on the left and slightly in advance of the 1st Missouri. A ravine (about 60 yards across) separated the two regiments. In crossing the crest of "Bloody Hill," the Kansans were exposed to an enfilading fire from the Pulaski Arkansas Battery. The Confederates, however, were putting too much elevation on their pieces. Consequently, the round shot from their guns went howling high over the trees under which the Kansans marched. At first, only six companies of the 1st Kansas were in close contact with the Southerners (Clark's and Slack's divisions and the remnants of Cawthorn's brigade). The remaining four companies of the 1st Kansas led by Maj. John A. Halderman were posted on the right of Totten's battery. Here, Halderman's detachment suffered severely from the fire of the Pulaski battery. When ordered to ·the front, Halderman's battalion took position on the left of the six other companies, "which had thus far borne the brunt of the battle."[16]

After Price had thrown Parsons' and McBride's divisions of the Missouri State Guard into the fray, Captain Totten reported that the fighting raged "in the thick woods and underbrush to the front and right of the position occupied by . . . [his] battery." When Lyon learned that the 1st Missouri was being hardpressed by Clark's, Parsons' and McBride's troops, he ordered Totten to advance one of his sections to Andrews' assistance. Taking charge of one of his sections, Totten moved forward. In addition to the crews serving the guns, Totten was assisted by Capt. Gordon Granger and Lt. David Murphy. These two guns were placed in battery in front of Colonel Andrews' right flank company. Within 200 yards of the position where the guns had been unlimbered was a Confederate regiment. The Rebel unit displayed two flags — one the National Emblem, the other a secessionist banner. At first, Captain Totten was uncertain of his proper course of action. He was afraid "that by some accident a portion of our own troops might have got thus far in advance." Totten's qualms were soon dispelled when the opposing battleline fired a volley at his gunners. The Yankees replied with canister.[17]

By this time, Lt. John V. Du Bois' provisional battery had reached the front. Since no position had been assigned him, Du Bois had his cannoneers unlimber their four smoothbore guns (three 6-pounders and one 12-pounder) on the eastern slope of "Bloody Hill" about 400 yards west of the Pulaski Arkansas Battery. (Du Bois' guns were about 70 yards to the left and rear of Totten's position.) Once his men had placed their pieces in battery, Du Bois had them open fire on the Arkansans' guns. Du Bois' gunners, in the ensuing duel, enjoyed a pronounced advantage over the Confederates. In the first place, Du Bois' battery was posted on higher ground; second, his men were partially and his horses completely in defilade and, therefore,, sheltered from the foe's musketry. So effective was the fire of Du Bois' cannons that the Arkansans were forced to shift position. Captain Woodruff's gunners moved their four pieces a short distance to the right.[18]

Captain Steele's battalion of regulars was posted in support of Du Bois' battery. [19] The 1st Iowa was drawn up in line of battle on the lcft of Du Bois' guns. Two companies (D and E) of the 1st Iowa were deployed as skirmishers and thrown forward. Throughout the artillery duel, the Iowans grimly held their ground. Private Ware recalled:

> Across . . . [Wilson Creek] which was not very far, perhaps one-third of a mile, a battery [the Pulaski] made a specialty of our ranks, opening out thunderously. We all lay down on the ground, and for some time the shells, round shot and canister were playing closely over our heads.
>
> Our company [E] did not have much to do for a while in the way of shooting; we simply laid down on the ridge and watched the battery . . . [to our right], or sat up or kneeled down.
>
> The duel was very interesting and our boys stayed close to the earth. Considerable damage was done to our artillery, but they were not silenced. One of the large roan artillery horses was standing back of the gun over the crest of the hill. A shell from the battery in front of us struck this horse and tore off its left shoulder. Then began the most horrible screams and neighing I ever heard. One of the soldiers shot the horse through the heart.[20]

Major Osterhaus' battalion was stationed on the extreme right of Lyon's battleline. The right flank of Osterhaus' command rested on a ravine that turned abruptly to Lyon's right and rear. Osterhaus had the task of keeping the Rebels from turning the right flank of Lyon's main line of resistance.[21]

The 2d Kansas, the other regiment that had accompanied Lyon's column, was held in reserve. Col. Robert B. Mitchell accordingly stationed his men on the hill west of and overlooking Ray's cornfields.[22]

81

The Battle from 6 a.m. to 8 a.m.

Price's Missourians quickly organized their battleline and pressed forward. By 6:30 a.m., the battlelines on Bloody Hill were established and the tempo of the fighting increased dramatically.

Plummer's force crossed Wilson Creek and entered Ray's cornfield around 6:30 a.m. Plummer observed that the Pulaski Arkansas Battery was having a telling effect on the Union troops. He therefore determined to take the Confederate battery. As Plummer planned his move, Colonel McIntosh was leading the 3d Louisiana and the 2d Arkansas Mounted Rifles toward Ray's cornfield and Plummer's position.

By 7 a.m., Sigel had crossed Terrell Creek, entered Sharp's cornfield and deployed his men in preparation to receive the South Kansas-Texas Cavalry's attack. Sigel bombarded the Southern cavalrymen until 7:30 a.m. when the Southerners fled. The way was now open for Sigel to continue his advance. Also by this time, General McCulloch had determined the size and composition of Sigel's force and was making preparations to attack him.

By 7 a.m., Plummer had made contact with the 3d Louisiana and the 2d Arkansas Mounted Rifles. A sharp fight ensued. McIntosh ordered the Confederates to charge. Overwhelmed, Plummer's force retreated towards Wilson Creek. The small Union force would have been overtaken if Du Bois' guns had not opened fire and dispersed Plummer's pursuers. The 3d Louisiana retreated southeast and regrouped behind the Ray house. From the Ray house, the Louisiana regiment marched down the Wire road to join the attack force McCulloch had organized to disperse Sigel.

By 7:30 a.m., McBride's Division had launched a determined attack on the right flank of Lyon's line on "Bloody Hill." By 8 a.m., the flanking movement had petered out and Price recalled McBride.

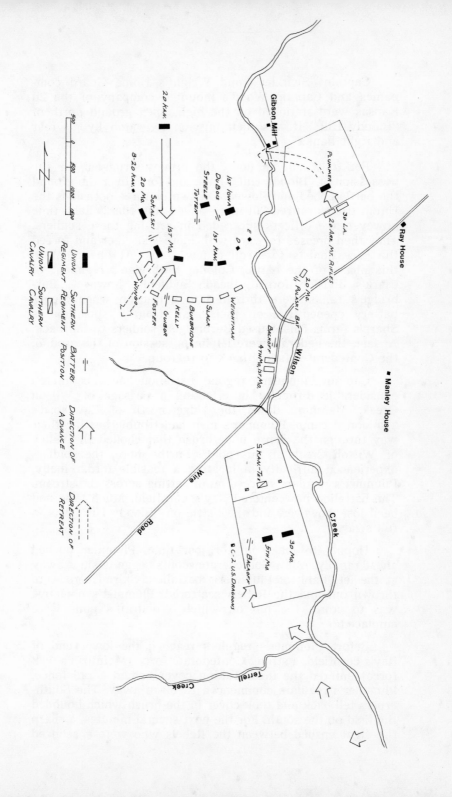

Gibson Mill

Plummer

2D ARK. MT. RIFLES

3D LA.

Ray House

Manley House

2 KAN.

B-2D KAN.

2D MO.

SOKALSKI

1ST IOWA

DuBos

STEELE

TOTTEN

1ST KAN.

1ST MO.

WINGO

FOSTER

GUIBOR

KELLY

BURBRIDGE

SLACK

WEIGHTMAN

2D MO.

PULASKI BAT.

Wilson

BACKOFF

4TH MO., 1ST MO.

Wire

Road

S. KAN.-TEX.

D.C.-2 U.S. DRAGOONS

BACKOFF

3D MO.

5TH MO.

Creek

Terrell

Creek

N

500   0   500   1000   1500

SOUTHERN REGIMENT POSITION

UNION REGIMENT POSITION

BATTERY

UNION CAVALRY

SOUTHERN CAVALRY

DIRECTION OF ADVANCE

DIRECTION OF RETREAT

Captains Switzler's and Wright's Home Guard companies and Captain Wood's mounted company of the 2d Kansas were stationed on the high, open ground north of "Bloody Hill." It was their mission to watch Lyon's rear and right flank.[23]

For fully half an hour, the armies struggled for the possession of "Bloody Hill." Back and forth over the ground the battle ebbed and flowed. On two or three occasions the Union troops retired "in more or less disorder." Each time however, the officers succeeded in rallying these soldiers. They then pressed forward with increased vigor and forced the Secessionists to recoil a few steps. At one point in this phase of the battle, Colonel Burbridge's regiment of Clark's division forged ahead. Suddenly, however, Burbridge's ranks were thrown into confusion when Sigel's battery opened fire on their rear, from its position as Sharp's farm. This caused Burbridge's soldiers to fall back. At last, the Federals were left in possession of the ground, the Confederates falling back to regroup.[24]

Captain Plummer's regular battalion had encountered considerable difficulty in effecting a passage of Wilson Creek. Marching down the ridge north of Cawthorn's abandoned camp, Plummer's men had trouble beating their way through the dense underbrush that choked the valley of Wilson Creek at this point. Furthermore, the soldiers experienced difficulty in locating a feasible ford. Finally, Plummer's regulars succeeding in getting across the stream. The battalion now entered Ray's cornfield. Much time had been lost, however, and the battle on "Bloody Hill" was in full sway.

Hoping to make up for lost time, Plummer pushed ahead rapidly. A few Confederate scouts began to snipe away at the left flank of Plummer's battalion. Skirmishers were thrown out and the Rebels scattered. Plummer's objective was to storm the hill on which Woodruff's guns were emplaced.[25]

Before Plummer's regulars reached the lower end of Ray's cornfield, a strong Confederate force (McIntosh's task force) entered the field. Taking cover behind a rail fence, Plummer's regulars commenced to blaze away. The Southerners fell back and took cover in the brush which bounded the field on the south. For the next several minutes, a sharp fire fight ensued between the Rebels who were ensconced

in the underbrush and the Yankees who were sheltered behind the rail fence. McIntosh, observing that the regulars'
fire was playing havoc with his men, ordered them to charge.
Leaping the fence, McIntosh led the troops out into the cornfield. The soldiers of the 3d Louisiana and about half the dismounted cavalrymen of the 2d Arkansas Mounted Rifles
followed McIntosh. Advancing relentlessly, the Rebels drove
the regulars from behind the rail fence. They pursued the
Federals across the cornfield and into a field beyond where
a crop of oats had recently been harvested.[26]

While the fight in the cornfield was in progress, a
Confederate battery (probably Bledsoe's) opened fire. After
the gunners had sent four or five rounds crashing into the
field, the battery commander realized that his projectiles
were undoubtedly as dangerous to McIntosh's task force
as to the foe. Consequently, he ordered his guns out of
action.[27]

Just before the Confederates launched their smashing
attack on Plummer's battalion, Du Bois' gunners had forced
the Pulaski Battery to cease firing. General Lyon, seeing
that the battery had accomplished its mission, sent Captain
Granger to order Du Bois to shift his guns to the right.
While the cannoneers were busy limbering up the left
section, they observed to their horror that McIntosh's Rebels
were driving Plummer's regulars before them. Granger
countermanded the order to march to the right. The gunners
swung their four pieces to the left. From this position,
Du Bois' artillerists were able to enfilade the Rebel advance.
Covered by the fire of Du Bois' guns, Plummer's troops
withdrew across Wilson Creek.[28]

Upon reaching the hollow where Cawthorn's abandoned
camp was situated, Plummer re-formed his battered battalion. Since the major had been wounded in the cornfield
fight and was no longer able to keep his saddle, he turned
over the command of the battalion to Capt. Arch Houston.
Captain Gilbert with part of his company did not rejoin
the battalion. Instead, he reported to Captain Steele.
Throughout the remainder of the battle, Gilbert's detachment served with Steele's battalion.[29]

The raking fire of Du Bois' battery checked the Rebels'
advance, and they in turn fell back in confusion. Colonel
Hébert passed the word for his Louisianians to retire into

the wooded area south of the Telegraph road. Confusion, however, reigned supreme. The regiment broke into several fragments. Maj. William F. Tunnard finally rallied the left battalion in an open field behind the Ray house. Lieutenant Du Bois was watching. He directed his gunners to open fire on the Louisianians. Du Bois' projectiles did not strike the Ray house. The chicken house, however, was hit. In response to the bombardment the Confederates displayed a yellow hospital flag. (The Ray house served as a Confederate hospital.) Du Bois then gave the order to cease fire. In addition to scoring two hits within the hospital area, the Union gunners had killed two and wounded several of Tunnard's men. Tunnard was forced to shift his assembly area. To protect his men from the fire of the Union batteries, the major re-formed his battalion under the cover of a hill in a field. Once the battalion had been mustered, Hébert appeared and took command.[30]

While Tunnard was reorganizing the left wing of the 3d Louisiana, Lt. Col. Samuel M. Hyams rallied the right battalion. Simultaneously, Colonel Embry re-formed the 2d Arkansas Mounted Rifles. Hyams and Embry marshaled their soldiers in a defiladed area near the ford.[31]

McCulloch, after sending McIntosh's combat team to deal with Plummer, had headed for Skegg's Branch. His purpose was to check on the progress of Sigel's column. Making a hasty inspection of the Confederate dispositions, McCulloch decided that any farther advance by Sigel was barred by Pearce's division and the cavalrymen who had been rallied in the woods on the north side of the branch. McCulloch now retraced his steps. The general wanted to check on McIntosh's attack. By the time the general reached the cornfield, McIntosh's task force had routed Plummer's battalion. Since the Union threat in this sector had evaporated, McCulloch decided to use the 3d Louisiana to spearhead an attack on Sigel. At this time, Sigel's brigade was posted near the Sharp house.[32]

Unable to locate Colonel Hébert, McCulloch contacted Colonel Hyams. McCulloch "ordered the regiment to face to the right and march by flank movement toward the ford." After sending an aide to relay this message to Colonel Hébert, McCulloch led Hyams' battalion (about 300 strong) down the Telegraph road. Once again taking leave of his regiment, Colonel McIntosh joined McCulloch. Wilson Creek was forded and the column moved into the narrow valley north of Skegg's Branch. Here, Hyams' battalion was joined by about 70 Missouri infantrymen led by Captain Johnson. Before crossing Skegg's Branch, Hyams deployed his command into line of battle. When these dispositions had been completed, McCulloch gave the word and the Rebels waded the stream and started up the slope leading to the Sharp house.[33]

Colonel Rosser, whose command would cooperate in the attack on Sigel, had already completed his preparation. Rosser's regiment and the 4th battalion were in position on the west side of the Telegraph road, north of Skegg's Branch. Captain Bledsoe's three guns (two 6-pounders and one 12-pounder) were unlimbered and commanded the area where Sigel had established his roadblock.[34]

It was about 8:30 a.m. Except for an occasional isolated shot, the firing had ceased. Sigel's troops, blissfully unaware of the gathering storm, took it easy. The officers and men were confident that Lyon's column had scored a smashing success. All they would have to do was hold the roadblock and gather in the defeated Confederates as they came flooding up the Telegraph road. The smoke of battle blanketed the area, and distant objects could not be clearly distinguished.

At this time, Doctor Melcher had ventured into the area in front of Sigel's battleline. Looking over the hill, the doctor saw a body of men (the 3d Louisiana) moving down the valley toward Skegg's Branch. These soldiers were apparently coming from the direction where the doctor had last heard Lyon's guns. Riding back to Sigel's command, Dr. Melcher reported that Lyon's men were coming up the Telegraph road. Several skirmishers corroborated the doctor's statement. Melcher tentatively identified one of the approaching units as the greyclad 1st Iowa.[35]

Sigel now sighted the newcomers. Not seeing their colors, Melcher suggested "to Sigel that he had better show his, so that if it **was** our men they might not mistake us." (Sigel's troops were not dressed in the regulation blue uniform.) General Sigel turned and commanded, "Color-bearer, advance with your colors, and wave them — wave them three times." As this order was being executed, Lieutenant Farrand, followed by his orderly, rode up. The two cavalrymen had been exploring one of the abandoned Confederate encampments. Among the souvenirs they had collected were two Rebel guidons which they proudly flaunted as they rode from right to left along the front of Sigel's brigade.[36]

The colonels of the 3d and 5th Missouri had cautioned their regiments **"not to fire"** on the troops then approaching because they were friends. Sigel had likewise warned the artillery. Everybody was surprised by this unexpected turn of events. The Germans of Col. Charles E. Salomon's and Lt. Col. Anselm Albert's regiments chatted away delightedly, and the color-bearers beckoned with their flags to the advancing legions to "come on."[37]

Not trusting his own eyes, Sigel sent Corporal Tod of the 3d Missouri to challenge the approaching soldiers. By this time, however, the newcomers had closed to within about 40 yards. When Tod appeared on the brow of the hill, McCulloch ordered Hyams' battalion to halt. McCulloch then asked Tod to identify his command. He replied, "Sigel's regiment." Evidently realizing his mistake, the corporal started to raise his rifle and shoot the general. But before Tod could pull the trigger, Cpl. Henry Gentles of the Pelican Rifles cut him down with "a messenger of death" from his Mississippi rifle. Turning to Capt. John P. Vigilini of the Pelican Rifles, McCulloch said, "Captain, take your company up and give them h--l." At this, Hyams' battleline surged up the hill on the double.[38]

The startled Sigel shouted for his men to open fire. It was too late, however. Now the Confederate artillery growled into action. From the opposite side of Wilson Creek, General Pearce had observed Sigel's advance. (Pearce had established his command post at the position occupied by the Fort Smith Battery.) At first, Pearce was unable to determine whether Sigel's column was friend or foe. But when a gust of wind unfurled his colors, the watching Confederates were no longer in doubt. Pearce accordingly directed Captain Reid to open fire.[39]

From their masked position opposite the mouth of Skegg's Branch, the cannoneers of the Fort Smith Battery enfiladed the right flank of Sigel's battleline. At the same time, Bledsoe's gunners delivered a frontal fire from their position on the south slope of "Bloody Hill." Doctor Melcher recalled that the artillery fire caused "a great deal of noise as the shot struck the fence and trees, but . . . [did not do] much damage, as far as observed, except to scare the men, who hunted for cover like a flock of your partridges suddenly disturbed."[40]

"The jabbering of the German soldiers was now something wonderful, but it had a different tone from that of a few minutes previously!" Sigel found it impossible to describe the consternation and frightful confusion engendered by this sudden attack. The cry, "They [Lyon's troops] are firing against us," spread like wildfire through the ranks. Most of the Union soldiers simply could not understand that it was the **Confederates** who were charging and firing upon them, grimly intent on sweeping them from the face of the earth. When the Rebel artillery growled into action, the Germans scurried about crying, some in English, "It is Totten's battery!" Others in German shouted, **"Sie haben gegen uns geschossen! Sie Irrten sich!** ("They are firing against us! They make a mistake!")[41]

**Colonel Sigel forcing his prisoners
to draw off his cannon at the Battle of Wilson's Creek**

At what point in the battle this particular incident occurred is not known for sure. It was either at Sigel's second position when he shelled the South Kansas-Texas cavalry in Sharp's field or more probably at Sigel's final position when he was routed by McCulloch.

The artillerists, all of whom were recruits from the infantry, had seen little service. Sigel accordingly experienced considerable difficulty in getting them to take their battle stations. On the right, the gunners manning four of the pieces feebly answered the fire of the Fort Smith Battery. (The other two guns were not even brought into battery.) Within 3 minutes, the drivers assigned to three of these guns bolted for the rear, taking the horses and caissons with them. Sigel's infantry refused to bring their rifles to the ready until too late. Indeed, they could not be made to stop running, let alone fight. Salomon cursed in German, in English, in French. Sigel alternately threatened, bullied, and coaxed. It was no use.[42]

Before the Louisianians reached the plateau at the Sharp house, Rosser's command crossed Skegg's Branch. Moving through the thick underbrush, Rosser's troops advanced **en echelon** on the Louisianians' right.[43] In compliance with McCulloch's orders, Colonel Brown had dismounted a portion of his regiment. He led his troopers forward to support the attack on Sigel's brigade.[44] While McCulloch moved against Sigel's front, Colonel McRae at the head of his reduced battalion converged on the Federals' left flank.[45]

Near the crest of the hill, Captain Vigilini halted his command. Followed by Sgt. William H. Tunnard, he raced forward to reconnoiter. The captain, topping the rise, was shocked to find himself about 15 feet in front of a section of artillery. Vigilini shouted for the gunners to identify themselves. Before they could answer, Sergeant Tunnard remarked, "Look at their Dutch faces." The two Confederates dived for cover. A moment later, the gun captains pulled the lanyards and two rounds went screaming overhead. Vigilini bellowed out the command, "Fire!" After firing one crashing volley, the Rebels charged the guns. Retreating into a cornfield, the gunners were relentlessly hunted down by Vigilini's men, as they sought to escape.[46]

On the left of Hyams' battleline, Lt. William A. Lacey of the Shreveport Rangers sprang on a log, waved his sword, and shouted, "Come on Caddo!" Up to the very muzzles of the cannons the Louisianians rushed, killing the artillery horses and those artillerymen who were reckless enough to remain by their pieces. Discharging their pieces into the faces of the panicky Germans, the Southerners forced them to take to their heels. Gaining a fence beyond

90

the captured field pieces, the Rebels blazed away at the rapidly retreating Yankees. Here the Southerners suffered a minor mishap. As a result of the smoke that partially blanketed the area, the gunners of the Fort Smith Battery did not realize that their comrades had forced Sigel's troops to flee. They therefore continued to shell the Sharp's farm sector. Before the cannoneers were advised of the changed situation, a shell from one of their guns had killed one and wounded another Louisianian.[47]

McRae's Arkansans came sweeping down on the Union left, just as Sigel's men started to give way in the face of McCulloch's frontal onslaught. As McRae's soldiers saw the first Yankees break and flee, they brought their weapons to the ready and fired one crashing volley. McRae halted his detachment, and formed his men so that they would be able to sweep the road. The Arkansans then sighted another body of men coming toward them. McRae commanded the newcomers to halt and identify themselves. In reply, they gave a rousing hurrah "for the South." The colonel told his men to hold their fire. It was not until after the greater part of the column had passed that McRae realized he had been deceived. He then shouted for his men "to fire!" By this time, the Federals had a good head start. The best that the Arkansans could do was to discharge a few ineffectual volleys at Sigel's rapidly retreating Germans. McRae now wheeled his detachment to the right and joined the Louisianians at the four captured guns.[48]

Rosser's Missourians also reached the Sharp house plateau close on the Louisianians' heels. While the Confederates were exchanging mutual congratulations, a scout rode up and told McCulloch that Sigel was re-forming his command astride the Telegraph road. The general called for Colonel McRae. He told the colonel to take his battalion and smash this new Union buildup. (McRae's three missing companies had just rejoined the battalion.) A short, rapid advance convinced McRae that there was no truth to the report. The Arkansas battalion thereupon returned to its camp on the east side of Wilson Creek.[49]

Within minutes after the rout of Sigel's brigade, several other Confederate units reached the captured guns. First came Colonel Brown's dismounted cavalry regiment. Seeing that his assistance was not needed, Brown recrossed Skegg's Branch. The colonel planned to rejoin his parent unit, Parsons' division.[50]

Next came Tunnard's wing of the 3d Louisiana, without two companies which had remained with Colonel Hébert. (Accompanied by these two companies, Colonel Hébert had advanced to the support of Price's Missourians on "Bloody Hill.") Following Tunnard's arrival, Colonel Hyams regrouped and mustered the regiment. When this business was taken care of, the Louisianians proceeded to roll three of the four captured cannons off the hill. Since the Louisianians had captured the fourth gun's horses, a detail drove it across the valley and presented it to the Pulaski Arkansas Battery. Colonel Hyams then marched the regiment down the hill and across Skegg's Branch. After forming his regiment into line, Hyams waited for Colonel Hébert to appear.[51]

General Pearce had watched the defeat of Sigel's brigade from his temporary command post at the Fort Smith Battery. As a precautionary measure, not knowing how badly Sigel had been defeated, Pearce called for Colonel Rector. The acting commander of the 4th Arkansas was directed to shift his men to the left and post them on the heights east of Wilson Creek. From this point, Rector's troops would be able to command the road along which Sigel had retreated. Rector accordingly faced his men to the left and marched them about a mile to the south. (Three companies of the 5th Arkansas accompanied Rector's unit.) He then deployed his Arkansans on the high ground near where Sigel's artillery had first gone into action.[52]

At least one of Sigel's officers, Lt. Emile Thomas of Company F, 5th Missouri, tried to rally his panic-stricken men. The lieutenant was assisted by Doctor Melcher. Suddenly, a mounted Confederate battalion (Captains Alexander's, Crews', and Staples' companies, reinforced by a detachment of Colonel Brown's regiment) cut across the Union line of retreat. For a moment the two commands gazed at each other. Then, as Doctor Melcher recalled:

> . . . came a terrible rattle of musketry, and a great hubbub and confusion in the direction of Sigel's command, which was just around a bend in the road, to our rear.
> In a twinkling, men, horses, wagons, guns, all enveloped in a cloud of dust, rushed toward us, and in spite of Lieut. Thomas' utmost efforts, Company F started with all speed **down** the . . . [Telegraph] road toward the Confederate cavalry. The latter, seeming to think that they were being charged upon, wheeled and got out of the way very quickly![53]

Sigel's column now divided. The right wing (the 3d Missouri) and one gun withdrew down the road along which the brigade had approached the Sharp house; the left wing (the 5th Missouri) retreated by way of the Telegraph road. Colonel Sigel accompanied the right wing; Colonel Salomon stayed with his regiment — the 5th Missouri.[54]

About the time that Sigel's brigade gave way, a large Confederate baggage train was wending its way slowly up the Telegraph road. The officer in charge of the convoy did not know that Sigel's troops had been defeated. Consequently, when he saw Salomon's soldiers beating their way toward the train, he had the wagoners wheel their vehicles around. Applying the whip to their teams, the teamsters headed in the opposite direction.

As soon as the mounted Confederates had recovered their wits, they moved to interpose themselves between the Federals and the baggage train. Since Captain Staples was the ranking officer, he took command of these assorted units. Racing ahead, the Rebels overtook and passed Salomon's troops. Staples then deployed his men astride the Telegraph road.[55]

In the meantime, Salomon's column had reached the first house beyond Sharp's on the Telegraph road. Here the Federals captured Doctor Smith, a surgeon in Rains' division, and a number of wagons. At Doctor Melcher's instigation, Colonel Salomon released Doctor Smith. The two doctors returned to the battlefield.[56]

Following the departure of the two doctors, Salomon's column (about 450 strong) left the farm and marched in a northwesterly direction. Before going very far, the soldiers discovered an abandoned piece of artillery. (This gun had been left behind by Carr's troopers, when the wheelhorse had been killed.) Not wishing to leave the gun, Capt. Samuel A. Flagg of the 5th Missouri detailed several of his men and the Confederate prisoners to pull the piece. Later, the captain succeeded in locating four horses. These were hitched to the gun. Before the troops reached the Little York road, however, the cannon was abandoned. After gaining the Little York road, Salomon's command returned to Springfield without further incident.[57]

Lieutenant Farrand's company of cavalry also found its way back to Springfield by way of the Little York road. Following the collapse of Sigel's brigade, Farrand's troopers found themselves cut off from any friendly force. The cavalrymen fell back in a southerly direction. On doing so, Farrand accidentally encountered one of Sigel's guides (L. A. D. Crenshaw). Forcibly detaining Crenshaw, Farrand proceeded to round up a number of stragglers from Sigel's debacle who were wandering willy-nilly about the area. When this business was accomplished, Farrand directed the guide to take him to Springfield, via Little York.

Before Farrand's small command had gone very far it came upon the gun abandoned by Salomon's infantry. The tongue of the limber was broken, one horse was missing, and one of the remaining three badly wounded. In spite of these difficulties, Farrand's troopers took the gun with them. Next, the lieutenant came upon a deserted caisson. At this time, he was accompanied by only three men. The rest of his command had gone on ahead. Farrand had one of the troopers open the caisson. Discovering that it was filled with ammunition, he determined to take the caisson with him. The lieutenant and his companions then "tried to prevail upon some of the Germans to assist" them in removing the wounded horses from their harness, but they refused to stop. After much difficulty, Farrand's party "succeeded in clearing the wounded horses from the harness." They then hitched to the caisson two fresh horses and a pair of mules that Farrand had obtained from a neighboring farm. The march was renewed. Two of the men drove the caisson, while the lieutenant and Sgt. John Bradburn led the horses. Overtaking Salomon's column, Farrand put two of the infantrymen in charge of the caisson. Accompanied by his three men, the lieutenant rejoined his command.[58]

As the retreating column neared Robinson's farm, Captain Flagg told Lieutenant Farrand that the team which was pulling the gun had given out. Farrand accordingly ordered the improvised team which was drawing the caisson unhitched. This team was hitched to the gun. Before leaving the caisson, the lieutenant had a detail destroy the ammunition.

After reaching Springfield, Farrand and Lt. Samuel Morris of Sigel's staff obtained a number of wagons. These were sent back along the line of retreat to pick up the wounded who had been left behind.[59]

Before reaching Terrell Creek, Sigel had succeeded in re-forming and consolidating the men of the 3d Missouri into four companies, in all about 250 officers and men. Taking their brass six-pounder with them, Sigel's command marched to Moody's Spring. Here, Sigel was joined by Carr's company of cavalry.[60]

From his position in the woods on the left of Sigel's roadblock, Captain Carr could see little of what transpired at the Sharp house. During this engagement, a number of artillery and small-arms projectiles sprayed the hillside without killing any of Carr's troopers. Like Sigel's unfortunate Germans, many of Carr's regulars believed that their friends were firing upon them. Finally, about 9 a.m. the question of which side was doing the shooting was rendered academic when one of Carr's noncommissioned officers told the captain "that one of Colonel Sigel's staff officers had brought an order to retreat." Since all the troops in sight were falling back, Carr did likewise. He quickly disposed his men to cover Sigel's rear.

In the course of the retreat to Terrell Creek, Carr's troopers were fired on by Staples' Confederates, who had taken position on a brush-covered hillside. The Federals beat off the Rebels, but lost the gun they were escorting, when the wheel-horse was killed. Abandoning the piece, Carr's regulars marched to Moody's Spring. (This was the gun which was ultimately saved through the efforts of Captain Flagg and Lieutenant Farrand.)[61]

Sigel, after cogitating on his next move, decided that it would not be a good idea to take the route pioneered by Salomon's troops toward Little York. The colonel was afraid the Rebels might cut him off from Springfield. He therefore decided to move down the Telegraph road until he reached a road leading northeast toward Springfield. When Sigel's column left Moody's Spring, it included, in addition to the 250 infantrymen (badly demoralized), 56 of Carr's cavalry, one gun, and two caissons.[62]

As the column moved out and ascended the hill south of Moody's Spring, Carr's troopers took the lead. Carr was instructed by Sigel "to remain in advance, keep his flankers out, and report what might occur in front." Next came a company of the 3d Missouri, followed by the fieldpiece and the two caissons. Behind the artillery came the rest of the infantry, the whole flanked on either side by skirmishers.

After the exhausted Federals had trudged ahead about 1½ miles, Captain Carr observed "a column of horse of at least a quarter of a mile in length moving towards the south on our right and filing into the [Telegraph] road in front." Word of this development was immediately communicated to Colonel Sigel. The colonel directed Carr "to take the first left-hand road." Fortunately for the Unionists, there was a road leading to the east at the point where Carr had halted his command. Accordingly, the Federals turned into this road.

Before the column had proceeded very far, Carr received a message from Sigel requesting him to hold down the pace of the march so that the infantry could keep up. Carr responded with the information that unless the column hurried, the Rebels would attack them while they were fording the James River. Furthermore, the cavalryman observed, "the infantry and artillery should at least march as fast as the ordinary walk of . . . [his] horses." Sigel agreed with the captain's contention.

The advance was then renewed; the cavalrymen held their horses to a walk. Reaching the James, Carr was surprised and pained to discover that the infantry had lagged behind. Seeing a large cloud of dust rapidly approaching from the direction of the Rebel camps, Carr "concluded that it was no time for delay." He waved his men ahead. After watering their horses, the troopers forded the river. Carr's regulars then marched eastward until the captain arrived at a point where he believed he could safely halt and wait for Sigel to put in an appearance. When Sigel failed to show up, Carr continued on to Springfield.[63]

His troopers had disappeared from view when Sigel's infantry reached the west bank of the James. The lead company of infantry quickly forded the river. While the gun and caissons were crossing the stream, the Confederates struck.[64]

After crossing to the north side of Skegg's Branch, Colonel Major's command had joined Major Chilton's battalion of the South Kansas-Texas Regiment. Taking charge of the combined battalions, Major had supported McBride's infantry. When the Union advance was checked, the aggressive Major wanted to charge the foe. The thick undergrowth on the southwestern slope of "Bloody Hill," however, rendered a cavalry charge impossible. Still looking for an opening, Major shifted his position. He deployed his Missourians and Texans on a hill opposite Osterhaus' battalion. Shortly thereafter, Major learned that Colonel Sigel, with about 400 men and one gun, was retreating down the Telegraph road. Accompanied by two companies of Texans (the Dead-shot Rangers led by Capt. Hinchie P. Mabry and the Cypress Guards commanded by Capt. Jonathan Russell) and the Windsor Guards of his battalion, Major started off in pursuit of Sigel.[65]

Beyond Terrell Creek, Major's command was reinforced by Captain Staples' "battalion." Pressing resolutely ahead, the Confederates overtook Sigel's column at the James River. Colonel Major, without a moment's hesitation, waved his men to the attack. This sudden onset was too much for the Germans' already badly shaken nerves. At close quarters, the Dead-shot Rangers' short-arms "did terrible execution." Despite Colonels Sigel's and Albert's words of encouragement, the soldiers scattered into the surrounding woods. A running fight ensued. Before it was over, the Southerns had killed, captured, or wounded the greater part of Sigel's command. Colonel Major reported, "Sigel and his men fought with desperation, but were unable to withstand the terrific charge of our gallant men, before whose deadly aim of Western men they fell like chaff. I succeeded in entirely routing the enemy, killing 64 and capturing 147 prisoners." Captain Staples captured the colors of the 3d Missouri, which were subsequently presented to General Price. In addition, the Southerners found themselves in possession of the brass six-pounder, the two caissons and several wagons.[66]

At Nowlan's Mill, four of Sigel's men "skulked under the mill-dam." When called upon to surrender by the Southerners, they refused to budge. Consequently, they were then riddled with buckshot. The next day (August 11) men lay scattered all over Christian County, dead or wounded. Prisoners were bagged in great numbers — "run down by the Texas rangers and driven in like flocks of sheep, as timid now as harmless."[67]

Sigel, however, succeeded in escaping. Subsequently, the colonel attributed his good fortune to his garb. He wore a blue woolen blanket over his uniform and a yellowish slouch hat, which caused him to resemble a Texas Ranger. After reaching the east bank of the James, Sigel and one of his men took refuge in a cornfield. The colonel and his companion remained in hiding while the Confederates combed the area. Seeing their chance, the two made a break. They were immediately recognized as enemies and pursued by a few horsemen whose number increased rapidly. It was a lively chase for about 6 miles. The Confederates, failing to close the gap, eventually gave up and returned to their camp.

At Mrs. Chambers' house, 4 miles south of Springfield, Colonel Sigel finally reined in his horse. After getting a drink of water, Sigel and his lone companion rode into Springfield. Sigel entered the city at 4:30 p.m., 22 long hours after his column had confidently taken the field.[68]

Sigel's flight from the Battle of Wilson's Creek gave rise to a wicked little stanza of the song sung in the Confederate camps after the battle:

> Old Sigel fought some on that day,
> But lost his army in the fray;
> Then off to Springfield he did run,
> With two Dutch guards, and nary gun.[69]

VI/Price Fails to Carry "Bloody Hill" and Lyon Is Killed

Following Plummer's retreat, there was a partial hiatus in the fighting on "Bloody Hill." There the 1st Missouri was closely engaged with McBride's and Parsons' divisions of the State Guard. In the face of the furious Confederate onset, the alignment of Colonel Andrews' regiment was "considerably broken." Colonel Andrews, observing that the firing was increasing in intensity on the right of his regiment, hurried toward the point of danger. The colonel was wounded before he reached his destination.

Reining in his horse, Andrews told Capt. Theodore Yates that he had been hit. In case the colonel became incapacitated, the captain would have to take charge of the 1st Missouri. If this came to pass, Yates was admonished to "keep the men together." Feeling faint, Andrews returned to the left and obtained a stimulant from Surgeon Cornyn. Shortly thereafter, the colonel's horse was shot from under him. In falling, the animal pinned Andrews to the ground. The colonel was freed from the dead horse by several of his men. This accident prevented Andrews from returning to the right flank of his regiment.[1]

On the extreme left of Price's battleline, McBride's division, in moving to the attack, swung too far to the west. Contact between McBride's unit and Parsons' division was broken. After crossing a small ravine, McBride's troops took cover behind a slight rise. Once he had completed his dispositions, McBride led his cheering soldiers forward.

As a result of the heavy undergrowth, he was unable to pinpoint the Union main line of resistance. Consequently, the division was forced to feel its way cautiously ahead. When McBride's troops gained the crest of the ridge west of "Bloody Hill," they were fired on by Totten's battery. This caused McBride's Missourians to fall back "in some confusion." Assisted by his officers, McBride quickly re-formed his soldiers. Resuming the advance, his troops topped the ridge a second time. Once again, the Southerners encountered the well-directed fire of Totten's guns. Unable to hold their ground, the Rebels again recoiled.

Undaunted, the Confederates rallied, preparatory to making another attempt to seize the commanding ground. This time, McBride's troops were not to be denied. In spite of the vigorous shelling by Totten's battery, McBride's soldiers occupied the summit. They then started to trade volleys with Osterhaus' battalion and Andrews' regiment that guarded the right flank of Lyon's main line of resistance. Almost immediately, a wild rumor spread through the ranks of McBride's command. According to this tale, the

Looking for a Friend

A common and tragic scene on all battlefields, it was probably seen repeatedly at Wilson's Creek.

Confederates had made a terrible mistake and were firing on their friends. This rumor, as was to be expected, "dampened the spirits" of McBride's Missourians "and produced a momentary indecision in their minds and those of their officers."[2]

In the meantime, General Parsons had launched a vicious assault on Colonel Andrews' regiment. After about 30 minutes' firing of the most desperate sort, the 1st Missouri began to pull back. General Parsons reported that "the enemy gave way and sullenly retired toward the summit of the high ridge toward the southwest and about half a mile distant." Observing this, Parsons issued instructions for Col. Joseph M. Kelly's regiment and Captain Guibor's Battery to follow the Federals. Parsons hoped to gain possession of this commanding hill since he considered it to be the key to Lyon's position.

Urged on by Lt. William P. Barlow, who was in temporary charge of Guibor's Battery, the artillerists quickly limbered up their four pieces. Closely trailed by a small group of infantrymen (about 40 in all) belonging to Clark's, McBride's, and Parsons' commands, the cannoneers started up the hill.

Near the crest of the ridge, the Confederates encountered a column (probably the 2d Kansas) hastening to Colonel Andrews' assistance. Before the Rebel cannoneers could place their guns in battery, between 10 and 15 foot soldiers had dashed forward. They took cover behind some large oak trees immediately in front of the Federals. Taking deliberate aim at the approaching Yankees with their "common hunting rifles," the Rebel marksmen sent one volley crashing into the head of the Union column. This caused the blueclad vanguard to recoil and take cover in the timber and thick undergrowth. By this time, the Confederate artillerists had unlimbered their four guns. Just as the cannoneers were getting ready to dislodge the foe, a horseman galloped up and called to General Parsons. He told the general that Guibor's Battery "was about to fire upon our friends." Parsons accordingly had Lieutenant Barlow shift his pieces about 100 yards farther up the ridge.[3]

The commanding knoll now occupied by Guibor's Battery adjoined the ground held by McBride's troops. "From this point the ridge sloped off gradually in all directions, and . . . [General Parsons] had a fair view of the armies around . . . [him]." To his right, the general could see large numbers of Union troops drawn up into line. When Parsons gave the word, the artillerists began to hammer these Federal formations. After 8 or 10 rounds, the Federals started to retire out of the "beaten zone." About this time, Parsons was reinforced by a detachment of cavalry led by Colonel Carroll.[4]

In the lull that followed Plummer's defeat, Col. Robert B. Mitchell of the 2d Kansas became very restless. Up to this time, his regiment had been held in reserve and had done nothing except cover Plummer's retreat. Mitchell, therefore, called for his second in command, Lt. Col. Charles W. Blair. The colonel told Blair to hasten to the right, and "ascertain from Lyon, Deitzler, or Sturgis" what his next move should be. Blair was to find out if perhaps the Kansans could be used to a better advantage at some other point on the battlefield.

While crossing the hollow where Cawthorn's deserted camp was located, Blair encountered a number of stragglers from the 1st Missouri making their way toward the rear. When Blair rode up to Lyon's command post, the general told Blair to have Colonel Mitchell move the regiment to the assistance of the 1st Missouri. Galloping back to within hailing distance of Colonel Mitchell, Blair shouted for the colonel to move the regiment to the right. At a word from Mitchell, the Kansans started toward the front on the double. Crossing the ravine, the regiment rushed to the support of the 1st Missouri. According to Major Sturgis, the Kansans "came up in time to prevent the Missourians from being destroyed by the overwhelming force [McBride's and Parsons' commands] against which they were unflinchingly holding their position."[5]

Following the repulse of McBride's and Parsons' troops, the guns fell silent on "Bloody Hill." The opposing generals took advantage of this situation to redeploy their commands. Price, upon learning that the timely arrival of the 2d Kansas had kept McBride's division of the State Guard from turning Lyon's right, determined to recall his command. "Old Pap" had determined to abandon his flanking movement in favor of a concentrated smash against the Union center. Any future effort to turn the Yankees' flank would be left to the cavalry. Staff officers were accordingly sent to recall McBride.

When the aide reached McBride's command post, he told the general to shift his division to the right. Moving to the east, Col. Robert A. Foster's regiment passed to the rear of Guibor's Battery. Colonel Foster's regiment continued to the extreme right of Price's battleline. The regiment took position on the left of Cawthorn's brigade. McBride's other infantry regiment, Col. Edmund T. Wingo's, was posted on the left of Parsons' infantry.[6]

After being driven from his camp by the fire of Sigel's guns, Colonel Churchill had re-formed his troopers on the north side of Skegg's Branch. Shortly thereafter, one of Price's staff officers directed Churchill to reinforce General Slack's Missourians. Before moving to the attack, Churchill ordered his men to dismount. After the colonel had detailed enough men to hold the horses, he found that he had about 500 effectives. Quickly deploying his troops into line of battle on the Telegraph road, Churchill gallantly led them up the southeastern slope of "Bloody Hill." As they worked their way up the hillside, the Arkansans were exposed to both artillery and small-arms fire. By 9 a.m., Churchill's dismounted cavalrymen were in position on the left of Slack's infantry.[7]

General McCulloch, following the rout of Sigel's column, determined to visit "Bloody Hill." When Churchill's dismounted troopers marched up the hill, McCulloch accompanied them. What the general saw convinced him that Price needed every man he could get to insure the defeat of Lyon's command. Returning to the valley, McCulloch encountered Colonel Greer. At this time, Greer was eagerly looking for a place to put into action the five companies that had remained with him. When McCulloch saw the colonel, he told Greer to see if he could turn the Federals' right flank. In addition, McCulloch authorized Greer to call upon any other cavalry command, not currently engaged, for assistance in carrying out this assignment.[8]

As Greer started up Skegg's Branch, he encountered Colonel Carroll's 1st Arkansas Cavalry. Greer accordingly told Carroll of McCulloch's plans. When this business was taken care of, Carroll's regiment fell in behind Greer's battalion. At Skegg's Spring, the cavalrymen turned to the right and started up the ravine which debouched into Skegg's Branch. Near the head of the hollow, Greer halted his column. So far, the Rebels had been able to make a

The Battle from 8 a.m. to 10 a.m.

After McBride's flanking movement, sporadic shots continued. By 8:30 a.m., firing on Bloody Hill had ceased.

By this time Sigel had established his position blocking the Wire road. As Sigel waited, McCulloch advanced down the Wire road. The 3d Louisiana and the 4th and 5th Missouri charged Sigel's position. The Fort Smith Battery opened fire and racked Sigel's line. In short order the Germans were put on the run. The threat to the rear of General Price's troops on "Bloody Hill" no longer existed.

By 9 a.m., Price completed his dispositions and launched a vicious attack along Lyon's entire front. The 1st Kansas was hard pressed and Lyon was wounded while rallying these troops. As the situation became critical, Lyon ordered the 1st Iowa and 2d Kansas into the battle. The 1st Kansas retired to recuperate. As he led the 2d Kansas to the front, Lyon was killed. It was then 9:30 a.m. The Iowa and Kansas troops pressed relentlessly against Price's line.

As 10 a.m. approached, Greer's cavalrymen launched their attack against the Union's right and rear. Greer's charge diverted the Federal's attention, allowing Price to disengage his troops. As Greer closed on Totten's battery, musket volleys and artillery shells dispersed his charge and turned it into a rout.

By this time, Major Sturgis had taken command of the Union forces. As he reorganized his troops, Price backed down the hill and regrouped his men.

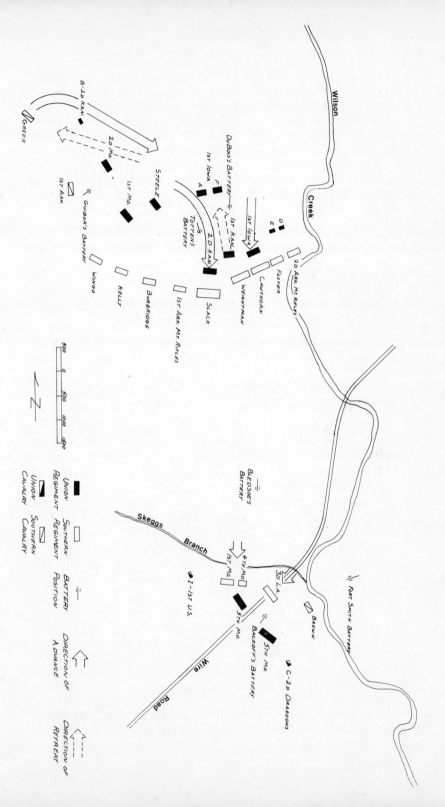

WILSON

Creek

DuBois's Battery
1st Iowa
F
A
Totten's Battery
1st Kan.
2d Kan.
2d Kan.
1st Iowa
D
E
Weightman
Cawthorn
Foster
2d Ark. Mt. Rifles

B-2d Kan.
Greer
2d Mo.
Steele
1st Mo.
1st Ark.
Guibor's Battery
Windo
Kelly
Burbridge
1st Ark. Mt. Rifles
Slack

500
0
500
1000
1500

N

Bledsoe's Battery
Skeggs
Branch
4th Mo.
1st Mo.
3d La.
I-1st U.S.
5th Mo.
Backoff's Battery
5th Mo.
Brown
C-2d Dragoons
Fort Smith Battery

Wire
Road

UNION
REGIMENT

SOUTHERN
REGIMENT

UNION
CAVALRY

SOUTHERN
CAVALRY

BATTERY
POSITION

DIRECTION OF
ADVANCE

DIRECTION OF
RETREAT

covered approach. Leading his regiment up out of the ravine, Colonel Carroll formed it into line of battle, facing east. (The hill currently held by the Arkansans had been previously occupied by McBride's soldiers and was now held by Guibor's artillerists.) While Colonel Carroll was deploying his regiment, Colonel Greer passed beyond the Arkansans' left flank. Once his battalion had reached a position where it overlapped the Federals' right, Greer halted. He proposed to take from the rear the gunners manning Totten's canister-belching guns.[9]

Crossing Wilson Creek in the wake of Plummer's rout, Colonel Embry led the dismounted troopers of the 2d Arkansas Mounted Rifles into position on the left of Foster's regiment. When the Arkansans went into action on "Bloody Hill," they held the extreme left flank of Price's battleline. Within a few minutes after fording the creek, Embry's troops were in contact with the foe.[10]

Colonel Hébert led to Price's assistance about 100 of his Louisianians, who had helped vanquish Plummer in the cornfield fight. Joining Slack's command, Colonel Hébert deployed his detachment on the southern slope of "Bloody Hill" within about 500 yards of Totten's battery.[11]

His disposition completed, Price ordered the attack to begin. It was about 9 a.m. as the Confederate officers led their cheering troops up the slope.

Simultaneously, Lyon had re-formed his main line of resistance. Steele's battalion, reinforced by Captain Gilbert's detachment, was called up. Steele's battalion of regulars had been covering Du Bois' battery. Reaching the front, Steele's soldiers were posted in support of Totten's guns. Preparations were made by the officers and men of Lyon's command to withstand a desperate onslaught. Already, the Federals could distinctly hear the shouts of the Rebel officers as they regrouped their troops.

Scarcely had Lyon disposed his men to receive the attack, before the Confederates appeared in force along his entire front. To make matters worse, the Southerners also threw out strong combat patrols which threatened the flanks of Lyon's battleline. Major Sturgis reported, "The engagement at once become general, and almost inconceivably fierce, along the entire line." Price's Confederates in places were massed in three lines, the front line lying down, the second kneeling, the third standing. The combatants loaded and fired their pieces as rapidly as possible. At times, the battlelines closed to within 30 or 40 yards of each other, as the Rebels surged toward Totten's battery, only to be hurled back by the determined Unionists.

Lyon, to hold his ground, was forced to commit every available man. For more than an hour (from 9 to 10 a.m.), the battle raged with great fury. The contestants were nearly equally matched. At times, the Federals would gain a few yards, only to see their gains erased by a Confederate counterthrust. This process would then be reversed. During this hour, "some of the best blood in the land was being spilled as recklessly as if it were ditch water."[12]

In this phase of the battle, the Union regiment on the left (the 1st Kansas) was particularly hardpressed by Weightman's command. In a desperate effort to recover the initiative, Colonel Deitzler led a sortie. Followed by Capts. Powell Clayton's and Bernard P. Chenoweth's companies and a portion of Capt. Peter McFarland's, Deitzler charged the attacking Missourians. Pressing down the hill, the Kansans rocked the Confederates back on their heels. The Kansans, before being checked, drove the Southerners (on a narrow front) back into the northern edge of their encampment. While leading this charge, Deitzler had his horse shot from under him and was himself severely wounded. Seeing that the Rebels were closing in on his combat patrol from all directions, Dietzler shouted for his men to fall back.[13]

Amid the noise and confusion of the constant firing, Captain Clayton failed to hear Deitzler's command to retreat. Instead, Clayton's company (E) continued to press ahead. Crossing the nose of a ridge, he sighted a body of men whom, from the uniforms, he took to be one of Sigel's regiments. The newcomers' line of march intersected Clayton's. The colonel in charge of the regiment asked Clayton:

> . . . where the enemy was. He [Clayton] replied by pointing in the direction of the retreating rebel forces, and immediately commenced aligning his company upon the regiment. All at once . . . [Clayton realized] that he was in a trap, and looking toward the colonel, he recognized in him an old acquaintance, being no less than Col. [James] Clarkson of "Kansas-Border-Ruffian" notoriety, ex-postmaster of Leavenworth.

In an effort to place some distance between his men and the Confederates, Clayton gave the command, "Right oblique, march!" Nothing happened until the Kansans had moved about 30 paces. Suddenly, however, the Rebel adjutant rode rapidly toward Clayton and commanded him to halt. In carrying out this order, he brought his company to an "about face" and confronted Clarkson's regiment. Next, the adjutant demanded, "What troops are these?"

"I belong to the 1st Kansas Regiment," replied Clayton, who asked in return, "Who are you?"

"I am adjutant of the 5th Missouri Volunteers," was the reply.

"What Confederate or United States?," asked Clayton.

"Confederate," the adjutant announced.

"Then dismount, G-d d--n you! you're my prisoner," Clayton said as he drew his pistol.

The Confederate sheepishly handed over his sword in response to Clayton's demand.

"Now," Clayton directed, "order your men not to fire, or you're a dead man." At the same time, the Federals started slowly to retrace their steps. To discourage the Confederates, Clayton forced his prisoner to stand between him and the rest of the Missourians. Collecting his wits, the adjutant shouted for his men to open fire. In response to the order, the Rebels started to blaze away. Hardly had the prisoner uttered these words before the aggressive captain shot him. A sergeant in Clayton's company ran the unfortunate man through with his bayonet. Clayton then shouted for his "men to run for their lives," which they did. Reaching the brow of a hill, Clayton re-formed his company.[14]

Since Colonel Deitzler had been wounded, Major Halderman took charge of the 1st Kansas. To encourage his battered regiment (which had started to recoil in the face of the slashing attack by Cawthorn's, Slack's, and Weightman's Missourians, Hébert's Louisianians, and Embry's Arkansans), Halderman galloped up and down the lines, waving his hat and calling on the soldiers "to remember Kansas and stand by the old flag." In return, the men cheered the major.[15]

In the meantime, Lyon had learned that the 1st Kansas had started to give way in the face of the sledge hammer blows delivered by the Rebels. Lyon accordingly directed the 1st Iowa to march to the Kansans' assistance. At the time that the marching orders reached Lt. Col. William H. Merritt, his regiment was posted on the left of Du Bois' battery. Covered by two companies (D and E), which were deployed as skirmishers, the Iowa battleline swept forward.[16]

Immediately after they had crossed the crest of "Bloody Hill" and started down the southern slope, the Iowans met the 1st Kansas "retreating in confusion." The Kansans broke through the right flank of the 1st Iowa's battleline. Companies A and F were separated from the rest of the regiment. Before Colonel Merritt could readjust his lines, his regiment was in contact with the foe. Confronted by a "murderous fire," the colonel shouted for his men to fall back and re-form. The din of the firearms and the yelling of the troops, however, drowned out the sound of the colonel's voice. Therefore, only the two right companies (A and F) obeyed Merritt's order. Six companies (B, C, G, H, I, and K) grimly held their ground and blazed away at the advancing Southerners. Expecting the remainder of his regiment to follow, Colonel Merritt had accompanied Companies A and F when they retired across the top of "Bloody Hill."[17]

Private Ware, whose company (E) was deployed as skirmishers, recalled:

> On the edge of the meadow . . . was a low rail fence; the Rebels rallied under the shelter of it, and, as if by some inspiration or some immediate change of orders, they broke it down in places and started for our artillery [Totten's Battery]. As they got nearer to us, their own artillery ceased firing, because it endangered them. When they got close the firing began on both sides. How long it lasted I do not know; it was probably 20 minutes. Every man was shooting as fast, on our side, as he could load, and yelling as loud as his breath would permit. Most were on the ground, some on one knee. The foe stopped advancing. We had paper cartridges, and in loading we had to bite off the end, and every man had a big quid of paper in his mouth, from which down his chin ran the dissolved gunpowder. The other side [the Rebels] were yelling, and if any orders were given nobody heard them. Every man assumed the responsibility of doing as much shooting as he could.

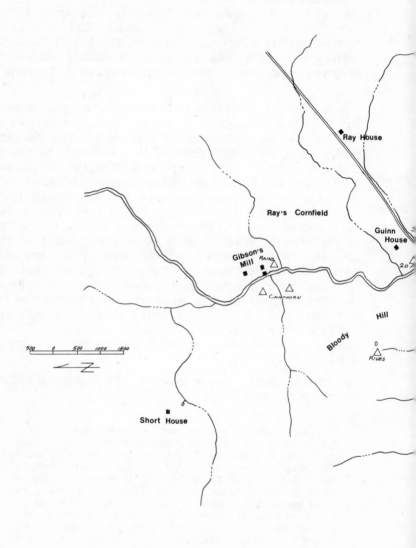

Ray House

Ray's Cornfield

Guinn
House

Gibson's
Mill

RAINS

CAWTHORN

Hill

Bloody

RIVES

500   0   500   1000   1500

N

Short House

The Wils
and the Location of

110

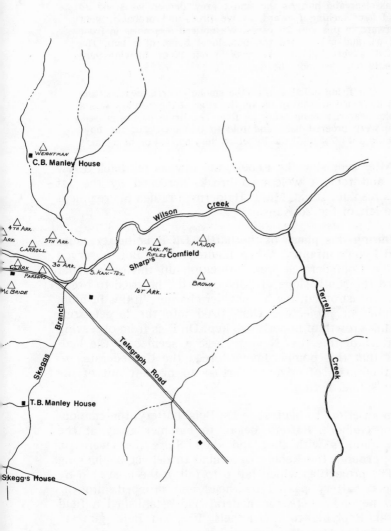

Weightman
C.B. Manley House

4TH ARK.
ARK.
CARROLL
5TH ARK.
CLARK
PARSONS
3D ARK.
MC BRIDE
S. KAN.-TEX.
1ST ARK. MT.
RIFLES
Sharp's Cornfield
MAJOR
1ST ARK.
BROWN

Wilson   Creek

Terrell   Creek

Skeggs   Branch

Telegraph   Road

T.B. Manley House

Skegg's House

ek Area
onfederate Camps

Finally, the field was so covered with smoke that not much could be known as to what was going on. The day was clear and hot. As the smoke grew denser, we stood up and kept inching forward, as we fired, and probably went forward in this way 25 yards. We noticed less noise in front of us, and only heard the occasional boom of a gun. The wind, a very light breeze, was in our favor, blowing very gently over us upon the foe.

Our firing lulled, and as the smoke cleared away, sitting on the fence in front of us, on the edge of the meadow was a color-bearer, waving a hostile flag. The firing having ceased, we were ordered back and told to lie down, but the boys would not do it until the Rebel artillery opened on us again.[18]

After repulsing the Rebels, the Iowans fell back a few steps and took a welcomed break. Screened by the 1st Iowa's resolute stand, Major Halderman rallied his regiment on the left of the 2d Kansas.[19]

During this phase of the battle, Du Bois' battery supported Lyon's infantry. When Lieutenant Du Bois observed that the Confederates were attacking up the ravine that scarred the south slope of "Bloody Hill," he tried to break up this thrust by cutting his powder charges. In this fashion, a number of projectiles were fired into the target area. The rank growth of underbrush kept Du Bois from observing the effect of this fire. Nevertheless, it seemed to the lieutenant that this bombardment forced the Confederates to shift their axis of advance farther to his left out of his battery's line of fire.

In an effort to neutralize Du Bois' battery, the cannoneers of Guibor's Battery began to hammer away at the Union gunners with shot and shell. Since they were on higher ground, the Rebels were able to deliver a plunging fire. The projectiles which failed to fall in the area held by Du Bois' battery passed overhead and dropped into the hollow beyond where the Federal had established a field hospital. Replying to the Rebels' fire, Du Bois' gunners "succeeded in partially silencing" it.

Throughout the engagement, Du Bois was "embarrassed by . . . [his] ignorance of General Sigel's position." On several occasions, Du Bois allowed Confederate units to form within a few hundred yards of his guns, because he believed that they might be Sigel's troops advancing to form a junction with Lyon's column.[20]

112

During this attack, Captain Totten conferred briefly with General Lyon. Lyon told the captain that he had been wounded in the leg. Totten also noticed that blood was trickling from a gash on Lyon's head. Feeling that perhaps the general needed a stimulant, the captain offered him some brandy, that he had in his canteen. Lyon declined and departed from the captain's battle station, riding slowly toward the right. [21]

On the extreme right of Lyon's main line of resistance, the infantrymen of the 1st Missouri, supported by Oster-haus' battalion, clung to their position. The slashing attacks of Burbridge's, Wingo's, and Kelly's regiments were parried by the nearly exhausted Federals. As the firing slackened on the right, Colonel Andrews encountered General Lyon. Andrews asked the general, "Have you seen or heard from our other column?" In answer to this inquiry, Lyon sadly shook his head. Observing that the general was limping, Andrews discovered that he had been wounded in the leg.[22]

During the initial stage of this attack, while General Lyon was walking and leading his horse along the line on the left of Totten's battery, the general's iron-gray horse had been killed. At this time, Lyon was trying to rally the 1st Kansas, which had been thrown into considerable disorder by the furious Rebel onslaught. The shell which killed the general's horse also wounded Lyon in two places, the head and the leg.[23]

Capt. Francis J. Herron of the 1st Iowa, who was within 20 feet of Lyon when this happened, stated:

> . . . he saw the horse fall, and that the animal sank down as if vitally struck, neither plunging nor rearing. Lyon then walked on, waving his sword and hallooing. He was limping for he had been wounded in the leg. He carried his hat, a drab felt, in his hand and looked white and dazed. Suddenly blood appeared on the side of his head and began to run down his cheek. He stood a moment and then walked slowly to the rear.[24]

When Lyon reached a less exposed position, he sat down. A member of his staff bound a handkerchief around the general's head wound. Seeing his adjutant, Major Scho-field, Lyon remarked, "I fear the day is lost."

113

Schofield replied, "O, no, General; let us try once more." In a successful effort to boost the general's morale, Schofield assured him that the troops could be rallied and that the disorder was of a temporary nature. Lyon, apparently convinced by Schofield's arguments that the situation was not so dark as it had first appeared, started on foot for the right. He was accompanied by one of his aides, who kept urging the general, in vain, to take his horse.[25]

Before going very far, Lyon encountered Major Sturgis. The major dismounted one of his orderlies and tendered his horse to the general. Lyon at first declined to accept the animal, remarking, "I do not need a horse." About this time, part of the 1st Iowa started to give way. Lyon accordingly directed Sturgis to rally the Hawkeyes. When Sturgis rode off to carry out this assignment, a horse was left for the general's use.[26]

As some of the Iowans were being led back into the fray by a staff officer, they called out, "We have no leader. Give us a leader." Lyon immediately asked to be helped on to the orderly's horse. As he straightened himself in the saddle, the blood from his leg wound was dripping off the heel of his boot. General Sweeny now rode up. Lyon, gesturing toward the Iowans, said, "Sweeny, lead those troops forward and we will make one more charge."[27]

Lyon, accompanied by Lt. William M. Wherry and six or eight orderlies, closely followed the progress of the Iowans' counterthrust. In doing so, the general's party rode on the right of the Hawkeyes. Before Lyon had proceeded very far, Lieutenant Wherry called his attention to a battle-line (probably Weightman's brigade) which was drawn up to the left and at right angles to the Iowans' line of attack. A group of horsemen were seen to ride out in front of this line. General Price (who wore a black "plug" hat) and Capt. Emmett MacDonald (who had sworn that he would not cut his hair until the Confederacy was acknowledged) were easily recognized. Lyon started as if to confront the Rebel officers, ordering his party to "draw pistols and follow" him. Lieutenant Wherry, however, remonstrated against the general's "exposing himself to the fire of the line, which was partly concealed by the mass of dense underbrush." The staff officer asked if it would not be better if he brought up additional troops. Lyon agreed. Wherry was directed to bring up the 2d Kansas. Pending the return

114

of his aide, Lyon advanced a few steps and joined two companies of the 1st Iowa (A and F) that had been detailed to hold an exposed sector of the Federal main line of resistance.[28]

In the meantime, Colonel Mitchell of the 2d Kansas had sent Colonel Blair to see General Lyon. Blair failed to encounter Wherry as he hastened to the point of danger. When he reached the general's command post, Blair told Lyon that the 2d Kansas was not presently engaged. In addition, Blair asked permission for the regiment to move to the front and occupy the crest of "Bloody Hill." "That is right, sir," Lyon replied, "Order the Second Kansas to the front!"[29]

Death of General Lyon

As General Lyon led the Second Kansas into battle, a volley of gunfire broke from the left. Lyon was struck in the heart and died as he slowly dismounted. He was the first general officer to be killed in the Civil War.

As soon as Blair rejoined the regiment, Mitchell led his cheering Kansans forward. The regiment advanced to the attack in column by platoons. When the head of the column passed Totten's battery, Lyon joined Colonel Mitchell. Swinging his hat, Lyon called out to the Kansas regiment, "Come on, my brave boys," (or "my bully boys," as some reports indicate), "I will lead you; **forward!**" [30]

After a short advance, the head of the column "raised the crest of the hill beyond the advanced [Totten's] battery." Here, it was ambushed. Among the soldiers cut down by this murderous fire were General Lyon and Colonel Mitchell. A ball penetrated Lyon's left breast, inflicting a mortal wound. Slowly dismounting, Lyon collapsed into the arms of his faithful orderly, Pvt. Ed Lehmann of Company B, 1st U. S. Cavalry. As he fell, the general exclaimed, "Lehmann, I am killed," and expired.[31]

Lt. Gustavus Schreyer and two men of his company of the 2d Kansas carried Lyon's body to the rear. Lehmann, bearing the general's hat and loudly bemoaning the death of his chief, followed. Before Schreyer's party had passed beyond the "line of file-closers," Lieutenant Wherry rode up and took charge of the situation. Apprehensive of the effect upon the troops of the general's death, the staff officer had the face covered. In addition, he ordered Lehmann, who was crying like a child, to "stop his noise." Wherry also tried in other ways to suppress the news that the general had been killed. In a sheltered spot near Du Bois' battery, the body was placed in the shade of a small blackjack. The general's features were covered with half of a soldier's blanket, and the limbs composed.

Surgeon Cornyn was summoned and asked to examine the body of the general. Closely scrutinizing the corpse, the surgeon wiped the blood from the side of the face. Next, he opened the vest and split the general's shirt, which was soaked with blood. Looking at the wound, Cornyn discovered it was in the heart. The aorta had been pierced. As soon as Cornyn had completed his examination, Wherry went to look for Schofield.[32]

The fierce blast of musketry that had struck down Lyon and Mitchell caused the lead company of the 2d Kansas (K) to recoil. In an instant, however, the soldiers recovered from their shock. Surging forward, the column deployed into line of battle to the left. At the end of 15 to 20 minutes' desperate combat, the Kansans drove the Missourians down the slope and into the brush beyond. Colonel Weightman was mortally wounded in this fighting. Having forced the Southerners to fall back, Colonel Blair re-formed his regiment on the brow of "Bloody Hill." Here the Kansans were exposed to a harassing fire from the Rebel artillery. Fortunately for the Federals, the Confederate

116

gunners were putting too much elevation on their pieces; the projectiles ripped through the trees overhead.[33]

Blair, who had assumed command of the regiment when Mitchell was wounded, now received a message from the colonel. Hastening to the field hospital, which was in the ravine north of "Bloody Hill," Blair saw the badly wounded Mitchell. The colonel told Blair "that he must take command, and fight the regiment to the best of his ability."

Blair answered, "I will try not to disgrace you or the State."[34]

About the time that Price's frontal assault waned, Colonel Greer's Texans moved to the attack. Screened by Colonel Carroll's Arkansans, Greer formed his five companies beyond the Yankees' right flank. When he gave the word, his troopers, letting go with a mighty "shout for Texas," thundered forward. This sudden onset caused the Union patrols operating in this sector to fall back. Some of the Federals fled without firing their guns, others held their ground until nearly ridden down by the Texans, then fired and fled. The men of Company B, 2d Kansas, which had been assigned to watch the extreme right of the Northern battle line, scrambled for cover in the brush and fired at Greer's troopers as they galloped past.[35]

When Captains Du Bois and Totten saw the Rebel cavalry charging toward their guns, they shouted for their gunners to shift their pieces. All of Du Bois' and several of Totten's guns were quickly wheeled to the right. The gunners then commenced to hammer away at the oncoming Texas cavalrymen with shot and shell. Simultaneously, Colonel Merritt ordered the two companies (A and F) which had rallied on Totten's guns "to about face." These sturdy infantrymen also started to blaze away at the Texans.[36]

Greer's attack, which had started off so gloriously, quickly collapsed when the Union artillery roared into action. Captain Totten made some caustic comments concerning the Rebel cavalry in his "After Action Report." The captain wrote:

> . . . the enemy tried to overwhelm us by an attack of
> some 800 cavalry, which, unobserved, had formed below the
> crests of the hills to our right and rear. Fortunately, some of
> our infantry companies and a few pieces of artillery from
> my battery [also Du Bois'] were in position to meet this
> demonstration, and drove off their cavalry with ease. This was
> the only demonstration made by their cavalry, and it was so
> **effete** and ineffectual in its force and character as to deserve
> only the appellation of child's play. Their cavalry is utterly
> worthless on the battle-field.[37]

Private Ware of the 1st Iowa witnessed the repulse of
Greer's attack. The Iowa infantryman recalled:

> About this time we heard yelling in the rear, and we
> saw a crowd of cavalry coming at a grand gallop, very
> disorderly, with their apex pointing steadily at . . . [Totten's
> guns]. We advanced down the hill toward them [Greer's
> troopers] about 40 yards to where our view was better, and
> rallied in round squads of 15 or 20 men as we had been
> drilled to do, to repel a cavalry charge. We kept firing, and
> awaited their approach with fixed bayonets.
>
> In the mean time, over our heads our artillery [Totten's
> and Du Bois' batteries] took up the fight; then the cavalry
> scattered through the woods, leaving the wounded horses
> and men strewn around. We captured several dismounted men
> by ordering them in under cover of a gun. A flag was seen
> lying on the ground about 150 yards in front of us, but no
> one was ordered or cared to undertake to go and bring it in.
> In a few minutes a solitary horseman was seen coming
> toward us, as if to surrender, and the cry therefore rose
> from us, "Don't shoot!" When within about 20 yards of that
> flag the horseman spurred his horse, and, leaping from his
> saddle, picked the flag from the grass, and off he went
> with it a-flying. The flag bore the "Lone Star" of Texas, and
> we didn't shoot at the horseman because we liked his
> nerve.[38]

Following their repulse, the Texans fell back and rendezvoused with Colonel Carroll's Arkansans. Greer's abortive
attack, however, was not a complete failure, because it
enabled Price to disengage his hardpressed troops. In the
face of the slashing counterattack launched by the 1st
Iowa and the 2d Kansas, the rebels were having a difficult
time. Once his men had fallen back, the aggressive Price
regrouped them preparatory to mounting another assault
on the Union main line of resistance.[39]

Shortly after he had fallen back, Colonel Greer noticed
that the firing to his right had abated. After watching the
Yankees' movements for several more minutes, Greer shifted
his command to his right. Here the colonel posted his Texans

and Arkansans in a fashion calculated to support the left flank of Price's battleline whenever "Old Pap" should renew the attack.[40]

Confederate Cavalry

Cavalry units were not engaged to any great extent at Wilson's Creek. The terrain and thick vegetative growth prevented effective movement. Greer's unsuccessful charge was the only cavalry display. For the most part, the cavalry was used to scout and carry messages.

VII/The Federal Retreat

When Lieutenant Wherry encountered Major Schofield, the major had just returned from leading a successful sortie by a combat patrol from the 1st Iowa. Upon being told of Lyon's death, Schofield announced that Major Sturgis should take command. En route to tell Sturgis of his elevation in command, Schofield stopped to view Lyon's body.[1]

The general had been dead about ½-hour when Schofield finally contacted Sturgis. By this time, the Rebels had fallen back and an uneasy quiet had fallen on the battlefield. When informed that the command of the army had devolved upon him, Sturgis was fully aware of the grave responsibilities that rested upon his shoulders. At this time, Sturgis reported, "Our brave little army was scattered and broken." To make matters worse, a yet undefeated Confederate force (which Sturgis erroneously estimated to number over 20,000 strong) was massed to his front. Most of the Union troops had been unable to refill their canteens since leaving Springfield 16 hours before. Furthermore, many of the unit commanders reported that their men were running short of ammunition. If the Confederates discovered this, the Army of the West would be faced with "total annihilation."

The great question in Sturgis' mind was, "Where is Sigel?" Sturgis felt that if Sigel's column arrived on the field and launched a vigorous assault on the Rebels' right flank and rear, then his command "could go forward with some hope of success." If Sigel had been whipped (which he had), there was nothing left for Sturgis to do but retreat.[2]

Confronted by "this perplexing condition of affairs," Sturgis called a council of war. This meeting was attended by the principal officers who were still able to take the field. All agreed that unless Sigel appeared soon, there was nothing left but to retreat, if indeed retreat were possible.[3]

The "consultation" was abruptly terminated when the officers sighted "a heavy column of infantry" moving down off the hill on the opposite side of Wilson Creek. Since the advancing troops came from the direction where Sigel's guns had been heard at the beginning of the struggle, the Union officers' spirits soared. A staff officer, who had been posted in front of where the meeting was going on, galloped up and called out delightedly, **"Yonder comes Sigel! Yonder**

Maj. Samuel D. Sturgis

Commander of the First Brigade

Sturgis became commander of the Union Army at Wilson's Creek when General Lyon was killed.

comes Sigel!" Sturgis, supposing that the newcomers were friends, told his officers to form their men for an advance. The staff meeting then adjourned; the officers hastened to rejoin their commands.[4]

Sturgis trained his fieldglasses on the approaching troops. On doing so, he observed that they "wore a dress much resembling that of Sigel's brigade, and carried the American flag." The major watched in fascination as the soldiers forded Wilson Creek and deployed into line of battle near the foot of "Bloody Hill."

Convinced that these soldiers were friends, Lieutenant Du Bois cautioned his gunners to hold their fire. This column was permitted to cross the ground covered by Du Bois' battery without being challenged. About the time that the newcomers (Gratiot's Arkansans) reached the defiladed area at the bottom of the hill, Sturgis' skirmishers raised the cry, "They are rebels." Seconds later, a battery (Guibor's) which had fallen in behind the column was wheeled about. Quickly unlimbering their four guns, the Rebel artillerists were pounding the Federals with shell and canister almost before the trails hit the ground. The infantry which had taken position at the foot of "Bloody Hill" now opened fire and slowly started to ascend the slope. Sturgis characterized this, the final phase of the battle, as "the fiercest and most bloody engagement of the day."[5]

During the lull that preceded this storm, the Union brass had made several changes in their dispositions. Major Osterhaus' battalion was shifted from right to left and posted in support of Du Bois' battery. Osterhaus' troops were joined here by the reorganized fragments of the battered 1st Missouri. Colonel Andrews of the 1st Missouri (who had been wounded earlier) had been sent to the rear by Surgeon Cornyn; Captain Yates now led the sadly reduced regiment. These units were charged with the mission of guarding the Union left.[6]

The 2d Kansas, reinforced by four companies of the 1st Kansas, held the Union right. Three companies of the 1st Kansas (B, F, and I) were posted on the right of Blair's regiment; Captain Clayton's Company (E) was stationed on the left. In addition, the 2d Kansas had been bolstered by the return of Company B, which had been on detached service. On the right of the 2d Kansas was a ravine. During the ensuing engagement, the Confederates used this gully as a covered avenue of approach.[7]

Totten's battery, supported by the 1st Iowa and Steele's regulars, defended the center of Sturgis' reorganized main line of resistance. Totten's guns were in front and to the right of the left wing of the 1st Iowa.[8] Steele's regulars were posted in front and to the left of Totten's battery. One company, Lothrop's, was deployed as skirmishers and occupied the crest of the ridge to Steele's left and front.[9] Three companies of the 1st Kansas held the brow of the hill on the right of Totten's battery. Another three-company detachment from the 1st Kansas watched the gap in the Union line between the 2d Kansas and Steele's battalion.[10]

Despite Lieutenant Wherry's precautions, news of Lyon's death was soon common knowledge. Private Ware recalled that during the lull:

> A big regular army cavalry officer on a magnificent horse rode down alongside of the rear of our company (E), and along the line. He appeared to have been sent for the purpose of bracing us up. He shouted and swore in a manner than was attractive even on the battlefield, and wound up with a big oath and the expression, "Life ain't long enough for them to lick us in."[11]

It was a little after 10 a.m. when Price's attacking troops broke contact with Sturgis' battleline and fell back to regroup. Except for several organizations that were pulled out of the line, the Confederate order of battle remained essentially unchanged.

On the extreme right, the dismounted troopers of the 2d Arkansas Mounted Rifles were recalled. An unfounded rumor was afloat that the Union cavalry was about to charge down the Telegraph road past the Ray house. Colonel Embry accordingly prepared to receive their attack. He deployed his men to cover the approaches to the ford. Since there was no truth to this report the Arkansans waited in vain for the phantom Union troopers to appear.[12]

When Colonel Hébert and his detachment of the 3d Louisiana fell back, the colonel was instructed by General McCulloch to regroup his scattered command. Once he had rendezvoused with Hyams' and Tunnard's wings, Hébert re-formed his regiment. Orders were now received by the colonel directing him to turn the Federals' right and take Totten's battery from the rear. Hébert then gave the word and the Louisianians moved off. It required a hard, difficult march on the part of Hébert's regiment to pass beyond the Yankees' right flank. Consequently, the tactical situation had changed drastically by the time the Louisianians gained the position from where Hébert planned to launch his smashing attack.[13]

Following his repulse, Price decided to recall Guibor's Battery. An aide was sent to relay this order to General Parsons. When the staff officer rode up, he directed Parsons to report to General Price with his battery and its supporting infantry. Since the battery occupied a commanding position from which it could shell the Union main line of resistance, Parsons questioned the wisdom of giving it up. Nevertheless, he moved to carry out Price's order. Leaving Carroll's cavalry to hold the hill, Parsons led his battery down the ridge. While his troops were retiring down the hill, a strong Union combat patrol dashed out of the underbrush to the column's left and rear. Closing to within about 40 yards of Parsons' rear guard, the Yankees discharged one crashing volley. Since the Rebels were moving down the hill, the Northerners overshot their mark. Consequently, not a man nor horse was hit. Before the Federals could reload, Parsóns' detachment took cover.[14]

Reporting to Price, Parsons was directed to place Guibor's Battery on the left of General Slack's command; General Clark's division would be on the left of the gunners. Guibor's battery was planted "within musket-range of an unidentified line of battle, which held the crest of "Bloody Hill." While the gun captains were laying their pieces, Parsons was told to have them hold their fire. Some of the Rebel officers, it seems, insisted that Guibor's artillerists were about to blast their comrades. Parsons accordingly shouted for the cannoneers to hold their fire until the troops to their front could be properly identified. Simultaneously, Clark's, Gratiot's, and Slack's infantry moved to the attack. Moments later, Du Bois' and Totten's battery roared into action. Satisfied that the Federals held the hillside to his front, Parsons gave Lieutenant Barlow the go-ahead. The Confederate artillerists returned the Yankees' fire with shell and canister.[15]

Up until this time (10 a.m.), Pearce's three infantry regiments had not fired a shot. Neither had Brashear's regiment of Weightman's brigade. Instead of following

Weightman into battle, Brashear's soldiers had been posted in support of the Pulaski Battery. These four infantry regiments, totaling more than 2,000 officers and men, had remained east of Wilson Creek throughout the morning while Price's men had struggled, in vain, to drive the Yankees from "Bloody Hill." These troops had initially served a purpose, but that was before Plummer's battalion had been vanquished in the cornfield fight and Sigel's column routed by McCulloch's attack. Now, however, they had nothing to do.[16]

Throughout the morning, General Pearce had closely scanned the slopes of "Bloody Hill" "for signs of victory." Instead of seeing his comrades sweep all before them, Pearce was disappointed to observe that:

> Totten's battery seemed to belch forth with renewed vigor, and was advanced once or twice in its position. The [Confederate] line of battle on our left was shortening, and the fortunes of war appeared to be sending many of our gallant officers and soldiers to their death. There was no demoralization — no signs of wavering or retreat, but it was an hour of great anxiety and suspense.

A little after 10 a.m., Colonel McIntosh galloped up to Pearce's command post with a message from General McCulloch. McIntosh informed Pearce that the Federals were exerting heavy pressure on the right flank of Price's battleline. Capt. Colton Greene, who was a member of Price's staff, reached Pearce's headquarters close on McIntosh's heels. He likewise urged Pearce to come to Price's assistance. At this hour, the officers told Pearce, "General Lyon was in possession of . . . [Bloody Hill"]; his lines were forward, his batteries aggressive, and his charges impetuous."[17]

Pearce realized that the "fortunes of the day were balanced in the scale, and something must be done or the battle was lost." Furthermore, his Arkansans were fresh and eager for a fight. Pearce accordingly told McIntosh to take charge of seven companies of the 5th Arkansas and the Fort Smith Battery.[18]

While McIntosh was marshaling these two units and getting ready to lead them to Price's assistance, Pearce proceeded to Colonel Gratiot's command post. Addressing Gratiot, Pearce told the colonel to take his regiment, the 3d Arkansas, and march to the point of danger. At an order from Gratiot, the men of the 3d Arkansas fell in and moved off in column of fours. Led by the general and the colonel, the soldiers forded Wilson Creek. Shortly after the Arkansans reached the west side of the stream, they were joined by General Price. "Old Pap" pointed out to Pearce and Gratiot the placed he wanted them to deploy the 3d Arkansas. The position indicated was on the left of Colonel Wingo's regiment. Gratiot's soldiers would go into action on the extreme left of the Rebel battleline.[19]

Price volunteered to guide the Arkansans to the ground they were destined to occupy. Throughout most of their approach march, Gratiot's soldiers were within range of the Yankees' artillery. The Federals, however, being uncertain of the Arkansans' identity, held their fire. As Price led the regiment up the southwestern slope of "Bloody Hill," he announced to the soldiers, "You will soon be in a pretty hot place . . . but I will be near you, and I will take care of you; keep as cool as the inside of a cucumber and give them thunder." Turning to Gratiot, who had served under him in the Mexican War, Price remarked, "That's your position, colonel; take it and hold it whatever you do. I will see that you are not too hard-pressed. Don't yield an inch."[20]

The Union skirmishers now opened fire on the head of the column. Gratiot deployed his men into line of battle. When this business was taken care of, the advance was resumed. About 50 paces had been covered when the Arkansans were suddenly assailed by a strong force of Federals (the 2d Kansas) in front and on the left flank. Shortly thereafter, several Union guns (Sokalski's section) roared into action. Playing upon the Arkansans' left flank, the Yankee cannoneers enfiladed Gratiot's regiment with shell and canister. To escape annihilation, the Arkansans lay down. Gratiot's soldiers, from the prone position, returned the Northerners' fire. For at least ½-hour, this deadly contest between the 3d Arkansas and the 2d Kansas continued. To make matters worse, Gratiot's men were also fired on by some unidentified Confederate soldiers who were posted behind them and lower down the hill.[21]

During the approximately 30 minutes the 3d Arkansas was engaged, the regiment lost a fifth of its strength — 110 killed, wounded, and missing out of 571 engaged. Despite these heavy casualties, the regiment grimly clung to its ground.[22]

Immediately after the 3d Arkansas had gone into action, Colonel McIntosh brought up the 5th Arkansas and Reid's battery. McIntosh put the seven companies of the 5th Arkansas into line on the right of Gratiot's soldiers. General Pearce, in his "After Action Report," commended McIntosh's conduct. The general wrote:

> I deem it lost time for me to attempt to sound the praises of the brave and chivalrous McIntosh. Always in the midst of the fight cheering and leading his men forward to victory, his name and conduct were a host in our behalf.[23]

When Price's tired Missourians and Churchill's dismounted troopers saw Gratiot's troops move to the attack, they began to cheer lustily. Urged on by their leaders, they started up "Bloody Hill." Within a few minutes, the fighting had again flared up along the entire front, which was not more than 1,000 yards in length. Already the Missouri State Guard had failed in two attempts to drive the Yankees from the hill. But this time they felt confident; they had been heavily reinforced.[24]

On the Union left, Du Bois' battery (supported by Osterhaus' battalion and the rallied portions of the 1st Missouri) held firm. Du Bois' gunners engaged Guibor's Battery in a deadly duel. When the Southerners found their ammunition running short, they were forced to cease firing. Captain Reid's Fort Smith Battery moved into position on Guibor's left. Once they had unlimbered their pieces, the Arkansans began to shell the Union main line of resistance. After Captain Reid's gunners had been in action about 5 minutes, Colonel McIntosh told them to cease firing.[25]

When General Parsons learned that Guibor's Battery had exhausted its ammunition, he ordered Lieutenant Barlow to withdraw the guns. Crossing Wilson Creek, Barlow parked his fieldpieces near the Guinn house. The lieutenant contacted Captain Woodruff here. The captain arranged to have the limbers of the Missouri battery refilled. While this operation was taking place, intelligence began to flow into Confederate headquarters indicating that the Federals had started to shift to the right. (Though the Rebel brass did not know it at the time, there was no truth to this report.) Accordingly, Parsons ordered Lieutenant Barlow to place his guns in battery on the high ridge south of General Pearce's encampment. Barlow proceeded to carry out Parsons' instructions. After considerable difficulty, the cannoneers unlimbered their four guns on the commanding knoll where Sigel had first attacked the camps of the Confederate cavalry. Colonel Rector's reinforced regiment supported Guibor's Battery.[26]

Having disposed of the Rebel artillery, Du Bois' battery and its supporting contingents concentrated on the right wing of Price's attacking battleline. After a sharp contest, the Confederate infantry was repulsed.[27]

The Union center (held by Totten's battery, the 1st Iowa, and Steele's command) was the focus of the Rebel onslaught. The company of skirmishers led by Lieutenant Lothrop (which Steele had thrown forward on the left) was driven in by the Missourians as they surged up the hill. Following up their initial success, the Southerners moved against Steele's command and Totten's battery. A gun (probably one of Guibor's) that the Rebels had emplaced below the crest of the hill to Steele's left and front, supported the attack. The cannoneers used both shell and canister, with what Steele described as "with more moral effect than danger to us." Within several minutes, the Rebels increased the strength of their battery. Steele reported that they "threw an incessant shower of missiles at us; but my men were ordered to stoop, and very few took effect upon us."[28]

Mistakenly believing that they had softened up the Union center, the Rebel brass sent a strong column charging at Totten's four guns. The Missourians closed to within 20 feet of the muzzles of Totten's pieces and received their charges of canister full in their faces. The clouds of smoke arising from the opposing battlelines commingled and seemed as one.[29]

During this deadly struggle, the left wing of the 1st Iowa was called up and took position at the guns. In response to a plea from Colonel Blair for assistance, Totten had sent Sokalski's section to the Kansans' support.[30]

Prior to this onslaught, Colonel Blair had been worried about the ravine which bounded his position on the right. This gully led toward the Rebel line, and gave the foe a covered approach to his regiment's position. Several scouts were sent to reconnoiter this ravine. When they failed to return, the colonel decided to investigate. Before Blair had proceeded 20 yards beyond his lines, he was fired on and his horse killed. Unhurt, the colonel scrambled back to his lines and obtained another horse.[31]

Immediately thereafter, Lieutenant Sokalski's section was seen approaching. In the meantime, Captain Chenoweth of the 1st Kansas had reconnoitered the ravine. The captain sighted a strong force of Rebels (Gratiot's regiment) coming up the hollow. Calling to Sokalski, Chenoweth indicated where he wanted the guns emplaced. Assisted by Maj. William F. Cloud and Capt. Bernard P. Chenoweth, Sokalski's gunners quickly unlimbered their two guns and began to blast the attacking Arkansans with canister. To protect his men from the Rebels' galling volleys, Blair ordered them "to lie down and load and fire in that position." Blair proudly recalled, "The fire upon us was terrific, but not a man under my command broke ranks or left his place."[32]

For the first time since the beginning of the battle, the Federal line never wavered. After the Rebel attack on the Union left had been repulsed, Lieutenant Du Bois limbered up a section to rush to Totten's support. Before Du Bois' gunners were able to clear a path through the wounded, the lieutenant received orders to fall back to the hill north of the field hospital.[33]

After about 30 minutes of close and deadly combat, the Rebels fell back to regroup. Just before the Southerners pulled back, Sturgis received a disturbing message from Colonel Blair. The Kansan reported that his men had nearly exhausted their supply of ammunition. Confronted by this grave turn of events, Sturgis issued orders for the Army of the West to retire. It was about 11:30 a.m. when Sturgis made this decision. The Confederate withdrawal, the major knew, would facilitate his efforts to disengage his command. Captain Granger and several others opposed Sturgis' decision to retire. They urged that the army fall back a short distance, regroup, and wait for news concerning the fate of Sigel's column. Sturgis reserved judgment, for the time being, on Granger's proposition.[34]

Once Du Bois' battery, supported by Osterhaus' battalion, had taken position on the designated ridge, the army started to pull back off "Bloody Hill."[35] When Colonel Blair received the order to retire, he announced that he "was humiliated beyond expression for . . . [he] felt that the battle might have been ours . . ."[36] In spite of his personal feelings, Blair proceeded to carry out Sturgis' instructions. Blair reported that his Kansans left the hill "in good order and slow time, with the men as perfectly dressed as on the drill ground." After crossing the hollow, Blair re-formed his troops alongside Du Bois' guns.[37]

Totten's battery, as soon as the disabled horses could be replaced, retired along with the 1st Iowa and the 1st Kansas. Steele's reinforced battalion covered the army's retirement. Before his troops were able to evacuate "Bloody Hill," the captain saw a strong force of Rebels advancing rapidly to the attack. Captain Granger had just joined Steele. Without a moment's hesitation, Granger rushed to the rear and brought up a hodgepodge of units (several companies of the 1st Missouri, three companies of the 1st Kansas, and two companies of the 1st Iowa), that had been supporting Du Bois' battery. Moving up on the double, Granger led these soldiers into action on Steele's left. Falling upon the right flank of the Rebel column, Granger's troops "poured into it a murderous volley, killing or wounding nearly every man within 60 or 70 yards." This caused the Southerners to recoil and discouraged any further thoughts of pursuit by these soldiers.[38]

After seeing that the wounded had been loaded into ambulances, Steele's command left "Bloody Hill." Du Bois' cannoneers covered Steele's soldiers as they fell back across the hollow. The guns were kept in battery until the last of the soldiers had passed, in what Lieutenant Du Bois described as "good order." When the battery limbered up their pieces and started to follow, the 12-pounder gun broke down. At Du Bois' request, Osterhaus' battalion remained with the battery until repairs had been effected.[39]

Following Steele's withdrawal, Sturgis' army marched unmolested and in tolerable order to the "high open prairie" east of Ross' Spring, which was about 2 miles from the battlefield. Sturgis called a halt here. The soldiers were permitted to refill their canteens and eat. Private Ware recalled that the men of the 1st Iowa ate part of their "big crusts." What was left over, the soldiers again slung over their shoulders.[40] Several wagons also arrived from Springfield loaded with bread. This bread was "devoured with a relish which extreme hunger alone can give."[41]

As soon as the soldiers had rested, Sturgis ordered the march renewed. At this time, the major "was undecided whether the retreat should be continued, or whether we should occupy the more favorable position in our rear, and await tidings of Sigel." This problem was quickly solved.

131

The Battle from 10 a.m. to 11:30 a.m.

After a short lull, Price was ready to begin another attack. Price's men advanced, made contact, and the final and most ferocious phase of the battle begun.

As Price's attack began, General Pearce was ordered to take the 3d and 5th Arkansas regiments and join Price on Bloody Hill. The sight of reinforcements spurred the Southerners on.

Guibor's battery exhausted their supply of ammunition and were replaced by the Fort Smith Battery.

Even though the Southerners attack was the most formidable of the day, the Union line held steady. The right wing of Price's line was dispersed by Du Bois' battery and the Union center was firmly held by Totten's artillery.

Du Bois' battery was ordered to take position on the ridge to the north of "Bloody Hill." The 2d Missouri supported Du Bois on the ridge. Sturgis sent the two units to the rear to provide cover if a retreat became necessary.

By 11 a.m., Price ordered his men to disengage and fall back. During the ensuing lull, Sturgis ordered the Union forces to retreat to Springfield. By 11:30 a.m., the Federals had abandoned Bloody Hill.

Price ordered another attack, but as the troops advanced they realized the Union forces had retreated and that the battle was over.

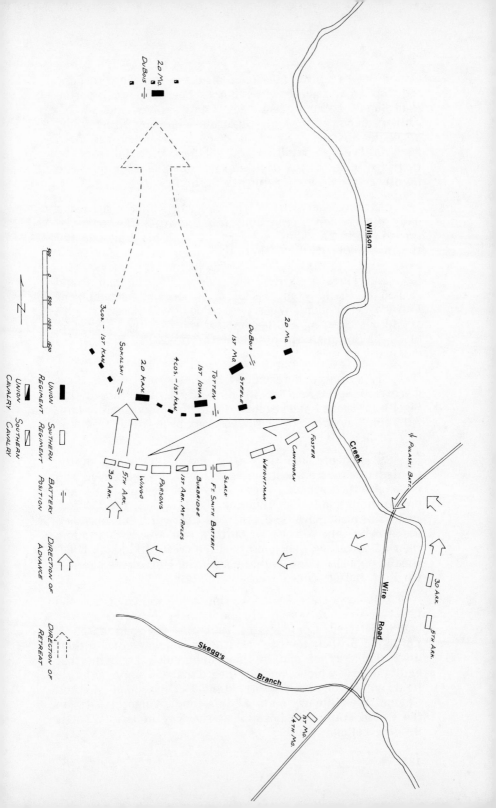

2D Mo.
DuBois

Wilson

Creek

N

500   0   500   1000   1500

20 Mo.
DuBois
1st Mo. Steele
Totten
1st Iowa
20 Kan.
4 cos.-1st Kan.
Sokalski
3 cos. - 1st Kan.

Foster
Cawthorn
Weightman
Slack
Ft. Smith Battery
1st Ark. Mt. Rifles
Bubbridge
Parsons
Wingo
5th Ark.
3d Ark.

Pulaski Batt.

Wire Road

3d Ark.
5th Ark.

Skegg's
Branch

1st Mo.
4th Mo.

UNION
REGIMENT
POSITION

SOUTHERN
REGIMENT
POSITION

UNION
CAVALRY

SOUTHERN
CAVALRY

BATTERY
POSITION

DIRECTION OF
ADVANCE

DIRECTION OF
RETREAT

One of Sigel's noncommissioned officers (Sergeant Fraelich) rode up on a foam-covered horse. The sergeant reported that Sigel's column "had been totally routed and all his artillery captured. Colonel Sigel himself being either killed or made prisoner." Since most of his soldiers had fired away all their ammunition and all the could rifle from the cartridge boxes of the dead and wounded, Sturgis now had no other option but to return to Springfield.[42]

Reaching the Little York road, the column sighted a body of horsemen approaching from the west. This command turned out to be Lieutenant Farrand with his dragoons and the piece of artillery that they had saved. Salomon's exhausted infantry plodded along behind the troopers. In his hand Farrand carried the guidon that he had found earlier in the day in the deserted cavalry encampment Farrand, Lieutenant Wherry recalled, "was received with vociferous cheering and became for the time the admiration of all, having marched around both armies and brought his command in safe."[43]

The march was resumed and the Army of the West re-entered Springfield at 5 p.m. Sturgis now learned that Sigel had escaped and reached the town 1/2-hour before him. All told, the Army of the West had been away from the city 23 hours.[44]

So suddenly had the battle ended that many of the Confederates were uncertain as to how the engagement had gone. Another attack by the bluecoats was expected and preparations made for it. Gradually, however, the Confederate skirmishers worked their way forward and occupied the ground where Totten's battery had stood. Continuing their advance, the Rebels crossed the crest of "Bloody Hill." On the opposite ridge could be seen the Union rear guard— Du Bois' battery and Osterhaus' battalion.[45]

This news caused a cry to ring along the front that the Federals were retreating. It made little difference to the badly battered Confederates that the foe had escaped. Springing to their feet, the Southerners gave vent "to their unspeakable relief and to their unbounded joy with that exultant cry which is never heard except upon a battle field where on the victors stand." This shout reached Colonel Weightman's ears. At this time, Weightman lay in the Confederate field hospital at the Ray house. "What is it?" the colonel inquired.

"We have whipped them. They are gone," one of his men replied.

"Thank God!," Weightman whispered.

In another instant, he was dead.[46]

In the meantime, Hébert's Louisianians had reached the head of the ravine in which Cawthorn's deserted camp was located. At this time, the Union rear guard was withdrawing sullenly across the hollow. Hébert hesitated to attack when he learned that there was an unidentified force on his rear. About 20 minutes elapsed before Hébert learned that these troops were friendly. He then moved forward. Reinforced by a detachment of Missourians led by Captain Johnson, the Louisianians swept to the attack. After a brisk skirmish, Steele's troops broke contact with Hébert's command. Hébert made no effort to press the pursuit. Recalling his troops, the colonel mustered and re-formed his command on "Bloody Hill."[47]

In the heavy fighting that had preceded the Union retreat, General Price had been wounded. Several times during the fighting, bullets had pierced the general's clothes. Finally, one of the projectiles inflicted a painful wound in Price's side. Turning with a smile to a nearby aide, Price said, "That isn't fair; if I were as slim as Lyon that fellow would have missed me entirely." Except for this officer, no one else knew until after the battle was over that the general had been wounded.[48]

Shortly after the Confederate skirmishers had occupied the top of "Bloody Hill," Generals McCulloch and Pearce, accompanied by several staff officers, met on the crest. At this time, the Pulaski Battery was engaged in a sporadic duel with Du Bois' battery, which was covering Sturgis' retreat. General Pearce recalled that the Confederate officers "watched the retreating enemy through . . . [their] field-glasses, **and were glad to see him go.**"[49]

The Southerners made no effort to pursue Sturgis' column. Several reasons were given by the Rebel brass for this failure. Like the Federals, the Confederates were plagued by an ammunition shortage. After the battle had ended, the camp followers, to whose presence with the army McCulloch had strongly objected, had robbed the dead and wounded of their arms and ammunition. This prevented the ordnance department from making an equitable redistribution of these items. In addition, McCulloch feared to risk a pursuit with his undisciplined command. Furthermore, rumors were prevalent that strong reinforcements were marching to the Unionists' assistance.[50]

It is certain, however, that Price wished McCulloch to pursue, but the latter would not. Price then resumed command of the Missouri State Guard, and then **he** would not pursue, for motives of his own.[51]

Probably the real reason that the Confederates did not follow the Yankees was that they had suffered such grievous losses themselves. The attrition among the ranking officers of the Missouri State Guard was terrific. Lt. Col. George W. Allen of Price's staff was killed while delivering an order; Weightman was borne to the rear, dying; Cawthorn and his adjutant were both mortally wounded; Slack had been fearfully lacerated by a musket ball; Clarkson was shot in the leg. Three regimental commanders (Burbridge, Foster, and Kelly) had been incapacitated by their wounds. Col. Ben Brown, the president of the Missouri Senate, was dead.[52]

Except for Colonels Greer's and Carroll's cavalry regiments, the Confederate troops (following Sturgis' retreat) were ordered to return to their camps. The two mounted units were directed to pursue "and capture a body of the enemy (Sigel's command)" said to be retreating in an easterly direction. After proceeding about 2 miles, it was evident to the Rebel horsemen that some other command had followed the Yankees. The mystery was dispelled when Greer's and Carroll's regiments passed Colonel Major's command returning to camp with a number of prisoners and the captured six-pounder. Greer's column crossed the James river and reconnoitered the Delaware road for some distance toward Springfield. Failing to find any additional signs of the foe, Greer's and Carroll's troopers returned to the battlefield about sundown.[53]

In the Battle of Wilson's Creek, the Federals lost 1,317 officers and men out of 5,400 engaged. Of these casualties, 258 were killed, 873 wounded, and 186 missing. There were about 10,200 Confederates engaged in the battle. The Rebels reported 1,230 casualties, 279 dead and 951 wounded. The Federals lost 24 percent of their personnel engaged, the Rebels 12 percent.

Besides the five guns (three 12-pounders and two brass six-pounders), the Rebels captured several hundred stand of small arms and a "quantity" of ammunition. The colors of the 3d Missouri also fell into the hands of the victors.[54]

Rev. R. A. Austin of Carrollton, Mo., was chaplain in General Slack's Division and summed up in a moving way the true tragedy of this and all battles. "It makes the heart sad to think of the hearts that have been lacerated with grief and the tears that are being shed; the ties that have been broken and the sufferings that have resulted from this bloody conflict. May a merciful God interpose and drive back the red cloud of war which hovers over us. May the Angel of Peace which has flapped her wings and left us, once more return to our beautiful and once happy country."

Southern Missourians driven from their homes

With the defeat of the Union troops at Wilson's Creek the way was open for Price to occupy Springfield and towns further north. Therefore, Unionists, fearing for their lives, left their homes and traveled with the Union troops to Rolla, Mo. The homeless refugees then waited for the war's end.

"Bloody Hill" from the East

Footnotes

NOTES ON CHAPTER I

[1] Return I. Holcombe and W. S. Adams, *An Account of the Battle of Wilson's Creek, or Oak Hills, Fought Between the Union Troops, Commanded by Gen. N. Lyon, and the Southern, or Confederate Troops, Under Command of Gens. McCulloch and Price, on Saturday, August 10, 1861, in Greene County, Missouri* (Springfield, 1883), 8.

General Lyon had left Camp Cameron (Camp Cameron was located at Boonville, Mo.) at the head of a column mustering about 2,350 officers and men on July 3. It had been Lyon's intention to rendezvous with a force led by Maj. Samuel D. Sturgis at Osceola, Mo. Sturgis' column, about 2,200 strong, had marched from Kansas City, Mo., on June 25. After the two commands had joined, Lyon planned to "proceed toward Springfield." Before leaving Camp Cameron, Lyon addressed a letter to Col. Chester Harding requesting that supplies be stockpiled at Springfield pending his arrival.

After reaching Springfield, Lyon planned "to co-operate" with Col. Franz Sigel's troops which were already operating in the "Southwest." Recent rains had caused the Grand and Osage rivers to rise. Consequently, the Union commanders were unable to use the fords. Instead, they had to ferry their troops across these two booming streams. It required 4 days to complete the passage of the rivers. In the meantime, Sigel had been defeated at Carthage on July 5 and forced to fall back on Springfield. *The War of the Rebellion: A Compilation of the Official Records of the Union and Confederate Armies*, Series I, Vol. III, 389, 394. (cited hereafter as O. R.).

Lyon's column consisted of:

	Officers	Men
Brigadier General and Staff	4	—
Company B, 2d U. S. Infantry	—	61
Battery F, 2d U. S. Light Artillery	1	60
Recruits, U. S. Army	1	134
1st Missouri Infantry	29	866
Two Companies, 2d Missouri Infantry	6	205
Pioneer Detachment	1	46
Artillery	1	13
1st Iowa Infantry	34	892
Total:	77	2,277

Colonel Harding, who maintained his headquarters in St. Louis, was the adjutant general of Missouri Volunteers.

[2] Holcombe and Adams, *Battle of Wilson's Creek*, 8; Thomas L. Snead, *The Fight for Missouri — From the Election of Lincoln to the Death of Lyon* (New York, 1888), 249-250.

[3] *O. R.*, Series I Vol. III, 394.
Sweeny held a commission as a brigadier general in the Missouri Volunteers dated May 20, 1861. Sweeny had reached Springfield on July 1 and had assumed charge of the Union troops operating in southwest Missouri. *Ibid.*, 15. Sigel's command (the 2d brigade, Missouri Volunteers) consisted of the 3d and 5th Missouri Infantry Regiments, and the 1st Battery, Backoff's Battalion Missouri Light Artillery.

[4] *Ibid.*, 394; Snead, *The Fight for Missouri*, 251.
The 13th Illinois, Col. John B. Wyman commanding, did not reach Springfield as Lyon anticipated. Colonel Wyman's regiment was detached, along with the 11th Missouri, to keep open the line of communications between Rolla and Springfield.

[5] *O. R.*, Series I, Vol. III, 395-396.

[6] *Ibid.*, 397.

[7] *Ibid.* At this time, Montgomery Blair was Postmaster General in Lincoln's cabinet.

[8] *Ibid.*

[9] Snead, *The Fight for Missouri*, 252.

[10] *O. R.* Series I, Vol. III, 399.

[11] *Ibid.*, 406.

[12] *Ibid.*, 408; Snead, *The Fight for Missouri*, 252.

[13] Holcombe and Adams, *Battle of Wilson's Creek*, 18.

[14] Snead, *The Fight for Missouri*, 252; *O. R.*, Series I Vol. III, 425.

[15] *O. R.*, Series I, Vol. III, 408.

[16] *Ibid.*

[17] *Ibid.*, 419

[18] Snead, *The Fight for Missouri*, 252.

[19] Holcombe and Adams, *Battle of Wilson's Creek*, 8-9

[20] *O. R.*, Series I, Vol. III, 44, 399. Sweeny's task force consisted of the 2d Kansas, a battalion of the 1st Iowa, Lt. George O. Sokalski's section of Battery F, 2d U. S. Light Artillery, two companies of regular cavalry, and Company I, 2d Kansas Infantry (Mounted).

21 *Ibid.*, 44.

22 *Ibid.*

23 *Ibid.*

24 *Ibid.*, 44-45.

25 *Ibid.;* Holcombe and Adams, *Battle of Wilson's Creek,* 9. Among the public property captured by the Federals were seven horses, a quantity of arms, munitions of war, flour, meal, sugar, sirup, salt, clothing, cloth, boots, shoes, hats, camp furniture, mule and horse shoes, etc. Except for the horses, most of these items were found in the courthouse. In addition, a quantity of lead was taken from a well into which it had been thrown. The arms and munitions of war were given to the Union Home Guards of Taney Couny; the clothing and provisions were issued to Sweeny's troops.

26 *Ibid.*, 406.
Sturgis' brigade included: Companies B, C, D, and I, 1st U. S. Cavalry; Company C, 2d U. S. Dragoons; Battery F, 2d U. S. Light Artillery; Companies B, C, and D, 1st U. S. Infantry; Lt. H. C. Wood's company of recruits.
Sigel's brigade was composed of: the 3d and 5th Missouri Infantry and the 1st Battery, Backoff's Battalion Missouri Light Artillery.
Andrews' brigade included the 1st Missouri Infantry; Companies B and E, 2d U. S. Infantry; Lt. W. L. Lothrop's and Lt. C. E. Farrand's companies of recruits; Lt. J. V. Du Bois' light battery; Maj. P. J. Osterhaus' battalion, 2d Missouri Infantry.
Deitzler's brigade was made up of the 1st and 2d Kansas Infantry.

27 *O. R.*, Series I, Vol. III, 407.

28 *Ibid.*

29 *Ibid.*, 409.   Besides reconnoitering the countryside to the west as far as Lamar and to the southwest to Carthage and Sarcoxie, Wright's Home Guards were kept busy threshing wheat. After being sacked, the wheat was sent to Springfield. There it was issued to the Army of the West.

30 *O. R.*, Series I, Vol. III, 411. The cantonment occupied by Sturgis' brigade was known as Camp McClellan.

31 *Ibid.*, 411-412.

32 *Ibid.*, 58.
The Federal officers in southwestern Missouri made an extensive use of scouts and spies in keeping track of the Confederate movements. These individuals marched in the Secessionists' ranks at times, hung around the officers' quarters, and picked up much useful information. They would then pass through the lines and carry this intelligence to Lyon or his subordinates. For the most

part, Lyon's scouts were residents of southwestern Missouri and knew the country like the palms of their hands. Generals McCulloch and Price, too, had scouts and spies, who kept them posted. In general, the Confederate scouts also hailed from southwest Missouri. Holcombe and Adams, *Battle of Wilson's Creek*, 11.

[33] *O. R.*, Series I, Vol. III, 58; Snead, *The Fight for Missouri*, 253.

[34] *O. R.*, Series I, Vol. III, 48, 58. Colonel Deitzler was in charge of one foraging party; Captain Carr was in command of the other. General Lyon reported his effective strength as follows:

Sturgis' brigade:

Four companies of cavalry	250	
Four companies 1st U. S. Infantry	350	
Two companies 2d Missouri	200	
One battery of artillery	84	
Total Sturgis' brigade:		884

Sigel's brigade:

3d Missouri Infantry	700	
5th Missouri Infantry	600	
Backoff's Artillery	120	
Total Sigel's brigade:		1,420

Andrews' brigade:

1st Missouri Infantry	900	
Four companies infantry (regulars)	300	
One battery	64	
Total Andrews' brigade		1,264

Deitzler's brigade:

Two Kansas regiments	1,400	
1st Iowa Infantry	900	
Total Deitzler's brigade		2,300
Grand Total, Army of the West		5,868

[35] *Ibid.*, 47, 49; Holcombe and Adams, *Battle of Wilson's Creek*, 11-12. The Hayden farm was located at Dug Springs.

[36] *Ibid.*, 49.

NOTES ON CHAPTER II

[1] *O. R.*, Series I, Vol. III, 611. McCulloch informed Walker that the aggregate strength of his brigade was 2,771 officers and men. The breakdown of McCulloch's brigade was:

3d Louisiana Infantry	868
1st Arkansas Mounted Rifles	768
3d Arkansas Infantry Battalion	277
3d Arkansas Infantry (State Troops)	626
Two Companies of Mounted Riflemen	156
Fort Smith Arkansas Battery	73
Total McCulloch Brigade	2,771

At the Battle of Wilson's Creek, McBride's division mustered 648 officers and men. McBride's troops were drawn from southeastern Missouri, from the swamps of Pemiscot and the cypress forests of Dunklin.

2 *Ibid.*, 622, 745.

3 *Ibid.*, 98.

4 *Ibid.*, 98, 622, 745.

5 *Ibid.*, 622-623.

6 *Ibid.*

7 *O. R.*, Series I, Vol. LIII, 717; Holcombe and Adams, *Battle of Wilson's Creek*, 10.
Rains was a well-known Jasper County politician. Rains' division was drawn from the populous secession counties of Saline, Lafayette, Jackson, Johnson, and Pettis.

8 *O. R.*, Series I, Vol. LIII, 717-718. When the Second Division took the field, the advance was protected by Carroll's Company of Arkansas Cavalry and the Pulaski Battery. Next came the Missouri State Guard. The Missourians marched in the following order: Parsons', Clark's, Slack's, and McBride's divisions. The 4th and 5th Arkansas regiments and the division wagontrain brought up the rear of Pearce's column. Steele's Third Division marched as follows: the 1st Arkansas Mounted Rifles, the 1st Arkansas Cavalry, the 2d Arkansas Mounted Rifles, and the mounted units belonging to the Missouri State Guard. *Ibid.*, 719.

9 *Ibid.*, 718.

10 *Ibid.*

11 *O. R.*, Series I, Vol. III, 98-99; Snead, *The Fight for Missouri*, 254.
As on the previous day, Carroll's troopers and the Pulaski Battery led Pearce's advance. The two Arkansas infantry regiments came next, followed by the Missouri State Guard. *O. R.*, Series I, Vol. LIII, 719.

12 *O. R.*, Series I, Vol. III, 745. General Clark's division was made up of men hailing from northeast Missouri.

13 *Ibid.*, 50..

14 *Ibid.*, 50-51.

15 *Ibid.*, 49, 51..

16 *Ibid.*, 47, 49.

17 *Ibid.*, 47, 49, 51, 58; Holcombe and Adams, *Battle of Wilson's Creek*, 12.

[18] *O. R.*, Series I, Vol. III, 51-52. General Rains had hoped to regroup his command at McCulla's Springs. (The advance guard had camped there on the night of August 1.) When he failed to find the expected reinforcements at that point, he retired to Crane Creek. *Ibid.*, 51.

[19] W. E. Woodruff, *With the Light Guns in '61-'65* (Little Rock, 1903), 36.

[20] Holcombe and Adams, *Battle of Wilson's Creek*, 12; Snead, *The Fight for Missouri*, 254.

[21] *O. R.*, Series I, Vol. III, 745. The man who died of sunstroke was H. D. Fulbright.

[22] *Ibid.*, 47, 58; Holcombe and Adams, *Battle of Wilson's Creek*, 12.

[23] *O. R.*, Series I, Vol. III, 48, 59; Holcombe and Adams, *Battle of Wilson's Creek*, 13.
Among the officers who attended the council of war on August 4 were General Sweeny, Colonel Sigel, Majs. Samuel D. Sturgis, John M. Schofield, Isaac F. Shepard, and H. A. Conant, Capt. James Totten, and Lt. G. A. Schaeffer.

[24] *O. R.*, Series I, Vol. III, 47-48.

[25] *Ibid.*, 48.

[26] *Ibid.*, 59; Holcombe and Adams, *Battle of Wilson's Creek*, 13.

[27] *O. R.*, Series I, Vol. III, 99.

[28] Snead, *The Fight for Missouri*, 225; Holcombe and Adams, *Battle of Wilson's Creek*, 55.

[29] Snead, *The Fight for Missouri*, 256.
McIntosh was graduated last in the class of 1849 from West Point.

[30] *Ibid.*, 256-257.

[31] *Ibid.*, 257; *O. R.*, Series I, Vol. III, 745.

[32] Holcombe and Adams, *Battle of Wilson's Creek*, 14.

[33] *O. R.*, Series I, Vol. III, 745.

[34] *O. R.*, Series I, Vol. LIII, 720; Snead, *The Fight for Missouri*, 258.

[35] *O. R.*, Series I, Vol. LIII, 720-721.
The Confederate infantry was scheduled to march in the following order: 3d Arkansas Infantry, 3d Arkansas Infantry Battalion, Weightman's brigade, Bledsoe's battery, Pearce's Arkansas State Troops, and the Missouri State Guard.

[36] *Ibid.*, 721.

144

37 Snead, *The Fight for Missouri*, 258; Woodruff, *With the Light Guns*, 37.

38 *Ibid.*

39 Snead, *The Fight for Missouri*, 258; O. R., Series I, Vol. III, 745.

40 Woodruff, *With the Light Guns*, 37-38. The Pulaski battery was equipped with two six-pounder and two 12-pounder guns. Bledsoe's battery was armed with one 12-pounder (Old Sacramento) and two six-pounders.

41 Snead, *The Fight for Missouri*, 259. Brown's regiment belonged to General Parsons' Sixth Division of the Missouri State Guard, while Major's battalion was attached to General Clark's Third Division of the Missouri State Guard.

42 *Ibid.*, Snead, *The Fight for Missouri*, 259-260; O. R. Series I, Vol. LIII, 435. General McBride reported that his camp was on the west side of the Telegraph road, "and about half way between the crossing of the creek and Sharp's residence." O. R., Series I, Vol. LIII, 434-435.

43 Snead, *The Fight for Missouri*, 260; Map titled, "Field of Battle of Oak Hill, August 10, 1861," *With the Light Guns;* N. Bart Pearce, "Arkansas Troops in the Battle of Wilson's Creek," *Battles and Leaders of the Civil War*, I, 298. The 3d Arkansas was encamped on the western side of the plateau, while the 4th and 5th Arkansas were bivouacked on the eastern side.

44 Snead, *The Fight for Missouri*, 260.

45 *Ibid.*

46 O. R., Series I, Vol. LIII, 427-428.

47 Snead, *The Fight for Missouri*, 261; O. R., Series I, Vol. III, 745.

48 *Ibid.*

49 Snead, *The Fight for Missouri*, 261-262; Pearce, "Arkansas Troops in the Battle of Wilson's Creek," 299.

50 Snead, *The Fight for Missouri*, 262.

51 *Ibid.*, 263.

52 Pearce, "Arkansas Troops in the Battle of Wilson's Creek," 299. On the morning of August 9, Captain Woodruff of the Pulaski Battery became apprehensive that the Federals might attack the Rebel encampment. He, therefore, thoroughly reconnoitered the terrain near his unit's camp. Woodruff, after completing his examination of the area, decided that the ground on the north side of the Guinn house would give his four guns a more commanding position. The

captain decided to get the opinion of the colonel of the 3d Louisiana, Louis Hébert, on the situation. Accompanied by the colonel, Woodruff again walked over the area. Hébert approved the captain's choice of ground. Woodruff, *With the Light Guns*, 38.

[53] *O. R.*, Series I, Vol. III, 99-100, 104, 746.

[54] Pearce, "Arkansas Troops in the Battle of Wilson's Creek, 299.

[55] Woodruff, *With the Light Guns*, 39.

[56] Snead, *The Fight for Missouri*, 263.

NOTES ON CHAPTER III

[1] Holcombe and Adams, *Battle of Wilson's Creek*, 13, 17. General Lyon maintained his private quarters in a house on North Jefferson Street owned by Mrs. Boren. His general headquarters were on the north side of College Street, a little west of Main, in the house owned by John S. Phelps. *Ibid.*, 17-18.

[2] *Ibid.*, 18-19.

[3] *O. R.*, Series I, Vol. III, 59.

[4] *Ibid.;* Holcombe and Adams, *Battle of Wilson's Creek*, 19-20. Captain Stockton was assigned to the 1st Kansas.

[5] *O. R.*, Series I, Vol. III, 59.

[6] Holcombe and Adams, *Battle of Wilson's Creek*, 21.

[7] *Ibid.*, 22.

[8] *O. R.*, Series I, Vol. III, 96.

[9] William M. Wherry, "Wilson's Creek, and the Death of Lyon," *Battles and Leaders of the Civil War*, I, 289.

[10] Holcombe and Adams, *Battle of Wilson's Creek*, 23.

[11] *Ibid.*, 23-24; *O. R.*, Series I, Vol. III, 57.

[12] James Peckham, *Gen. Nathaniel Lyon, and Missouri in 1861* (New York, 1866), 325; Holcombe and Adams, *Battle of Wilson's Creek*, 23.

[13] Peckham, *Lyon and Missouri*, 325.

[14] *Ibid.*, 326.

[15] *Ibid.* Lyon theorized that if the Rebels occupied southwestern Missouri, they would enforce a ruthless conscription policy.

[16] *Ibid.*, 326-327.

[17] *Ibid.*, 327.

[18] *Ibid.* Holcombe and Adams, *Battle of Wilson's Creek*, 21.

[19] Peckham, *Lyon and Missouri*, 327.

[20] *Ibid.*, 328; Holcombe and Adams, *Battle of Wilson's Creek*, 21-22.

[21] Peckham, *Lyon and Missouri*, 328.

[22] *Ibid.; O. R.*, Series I, Vol. III, 96; Franz Sigel, "The Flanking Column at Wilson's Creek," *Battles and Leaders of the Civil War*, I, 304.

[23] *O. R.*, Series I, Vol. III, 60.

[24] Eugene F. Ware, *The Lyon Campaign in Missouri — Being a History of the 1st Iowa Infantry* (Topeka, 1907), 310.

[25] *Ibid.*

[26] *Ibid.*, 310-311.

[27] *Ibid.*, 312.

[28] *Ibid.*, 313.

NOTES ON CHAPTER IV

[1] *O. R.*, Series I, Vol. III, 65, 81. Holcombe and Adams, *Battle of Wilson's Creek*, 29. Lyon's column consisted of Sturgis', Andrews', Deitzler's brigades. Sturgis' brigade included Plummer's battalion; Osterhaus' battalion; Battery F, 2d U. S. Light Artillery; Company D, 1st U. S. Cavalry; and Company I, 2d Kansas Infantry (Mounted). Andrews' brigade consisted of Steele's battalion; the 1st Missouri Infantry; and Du Bois' four-gun Provisional U. S. Battery. Deitzler's brigade was made up of the 1st and 2d Kansas Infantry Regiments. In addition, the 1st Iowa Infantry and two Home Guard units were attached to Lyon's striking force.

[2] Ware, *The Lyon Campaign in Missouri*, 314. On the Grand Prairie, there was no water and very little wood. It was possible to leave the road and move across the prairie at almost any point.

[3] *Ibid*, Holcombe and Adams, *Battle of Wilson's Creek*, 28-29.

[4] Holcombe and Adams, *Battle of Wilson's Creek*, 29; *O. R.*, Series I, Vol. III, 64, 75.

[5] Ware, *The Lyon Campaign in Missouri*, 315.

[6] *O. R.*, Series I, Vol. III, 60, 65, 73, 75. Dixie O'Connor, Personal Interview, June 30, 1960.

[7] Ware, *The Lyon Campaign in Missouri*, 315.

[8] Wherry, *"Wilson's Creek, and the Death of Lyon,"* 292-293.

[9] Holcombe and Adams, *Battle of Wilson's Creek*, 29; W. S. Burke, *Military History of Kansas Regiments* (Leavenworth, 1870), 3.

[10] Sigel, "The Flanking Column at Wilson's Creek," 304; O. R., Series I, Vol. III, 86, 89-90; Holcombe and Adams, *Battle of Wilson's Creek*, 29-30.

[11] Sigel, "The Flanking Column at Wilson's Creek," 304; O. R., Series I, Vol. III, 89.

[12] Sigel, "The Flanking Column at Wilson's Creek," 304; O. R., Series I, Vol. III, 89, 91; Holcombe and Adams, *Battle of Wilson's Creek*, 30.

[13] Sigel, "The Flanking Column at Wilson's Creek," 304; O. R., Series I, Vol. III, 86, 89, 91; Holcombe and Adams, *Battle of Wilson's Creek*, 30.

[14] Holcombe and Adams, *Battle of Wilson's Creek*, 30.

[15] O. R., Series I, Vol. III, 60, 65.

[16] *Ibid.*, 60, 65, 72. The 1st Missouri marched parallel with Battery F, "and about 60 yards distant." Shortly thereafter, Colonel Andrews deployed as skirmishers and threw forward one company (H).

[17] *Ibid.*, 60, 73; L. E. Meador, Personal Interview, June 27, 1960.

[18] O. R., Series I, Vol. III, 60, 65, 73.

[19] *Ibid.*, 127; Snead, *The Fight for Missouri*, 269.

[20] Snead, *The Fight for Missouri*, 269. Cawthorn deployed his brigade on the slope south of the ravine, where his brigade had pitched its tents.

[21] Burke, *Military History of Kansas Regiments*, 3; O. R., Series I, Vol. III, 60, 66, 82.

[22] Burke, *Military History of Kansas Regiments*, 12.

[23] Snead, *The Fight for Missouri*, 269-270; O. R., Series I, Vol. III, 60, 73, 75-76.

[24] O. R., Series I, Vol. III, 73.

[25] Snead, *The Fight for Missouri*, 271.

[26] *Ibid.*, 271-272; O. R.., Series I, Vol. III, 127.

[27] Holcombe and Adams, *Battle of Wilson's Creek*, 53.

[28] Snead, *The Fight for Missouri*, 272

[29] Holcombe and Adams, *Battle of Wilson's Creek,* 53.

[30] *Ibid.,* Snead, *The Fight for Missouri,* 272.

[31] Snead, *The Fight for Missouri,* 272-273; O. R., Series I, Vol. III, 100, 104-105.

[32] Snead, *The Fight for Missouri,* 273.

[33] O. R., Series I, Vol. LIII, 429.
Slack's division consisted of men from northwestern Missouri.

[34] *Ibid.,* 422-423, 425.

[35] *Ibid.,* 423.
Clark's division was composed of men from northwestern Missouri.

[36] *Ibid.,* 431.

[37] *Ibid.,* 432.
Three detached infantry companies led by Capts. Charles L. Crews, Thomas E. Staples, and Charles B. Alexander were temporarily attached to Colonel Brown's command.

[38] *Ibid.,* 435.
The encampment of McBride's Seventh Division, Missouri State' Guard, was on the west side of the Telegraph road, about halfway between the Wilson Creek ford and the Sharp residence.

[39] *Ibid.,* 427-428; Snead, *The Fight for Missouri,* 274; "Plat of the Battle of Wilson Creek," Position and Movement of Troops by Gen. Franz Sigel.

[40] O. R., Series I, Vol. III, 128; Snead, *The Fight for Missouri,* 274-275.
The 3d Regiment was led by Col. Edgar V. Hurst, the 5th was commanded by Col. James J. Clarkson. Major Brashear commanded the 2d regiment of Weightman's brigade on the day of the battle. Col. John R. Graves, the regimental commander, was not on duty during the battle.

[41] Snead, *The Fight for Missouri,* 274.

[42] O. R., Series I, Vol. III, 86-87; Holcombe and Adams, *Battle of Wilson's Creek,* 40-41; Sigel, "The Flanking Column at Wilson's Creek," 304.

[43] Holcombe and Adams, *Battle of Wilson's Creek,* 46.

[44] O. R., Series I, Vol. III, 89.

[45] O. R., Series I, Vol. LIII, 425.

[46] *Ibid.,* 433.

[47] *O. R.*, Series I, Vol. III, 118.

[48] *Ibid.*

[49] *Ibid.*, 109-110.

[50] Snead, *The Fight for Missouri*, 282.
There are two feasible places where Sigel's troops might have forded Wilson Creek. One is where the present ford crosses Wilson Creek several hundred yards south of the point where Terrell Creek debouches into the stream; the other is located about ¼-mile above the confluence of the James river and Wilson Creek.

[51] *O. R.*, Series I, Vol. III, 91.

[52] *Ibid.*, 87; Sigel, "The Flanking Column at Wilson's Creek," 304.
The Sharp house was painted white.

[53] Sigel, "The Flanking Column at Wilson's Creek," 304; *O. R.*, Series I, Vol. III, 87, 89, 91, 118.

[54] *O. R.*, Series I, Vol. III, 89.

[55] *Ibid.*, 91.

[56] *Ibid.*, 87, 89; Holcombe and Adams, *Battle of Wilson's Creek*, 41.

[57] *O. R.*, Series I, Vol. III, 87, 89, 91; Sigel, "The Flanking Column at Wilson's Creek," 305; Holcombe and Adams, *Battle of Wilson's Creek*, 41, 46.

[58] *Ibid.*

[59] *O. R.*, Series I, Vol. III, 87, 128; Sigel, "The Flanking Column at Wilson's Creek," 305.

[60] *O. R.*, Series I, Vol. III, 87; Sigel, "The Flanking Column at Wilson's Creek," 305; Holcombe and Adams, *Battle of Wilson's Creek*, 41.

[61] Holcombe and Adams, *Battle of Wilson's Creek*, 46.

NOTES ON CHAPTER V

[1] Snead, *The Fight for Missouri*, 276.

[2] Pearce, "Arkansas Troops in the Battle of Wilson's Creek," 299-300; *O. R.*, Series I, Vol. III, 121, 126.

[3] *O. R.*, Series I, Vol. III, 121, 124-125; Snead, *The Fight for Missouri*, 276.

[4] Snead, *The Fight for Missouri*, 276.

5 *Ibid.*, 277; *O. R.*, Series I, Vol. III, 123.

6 *O. R.*, Series I, Vol. III, 111-113; Snead, *The Fight for Missouri*, 277.

7 *O. R.*, Series I, Vol. III, 112.

8 *O. R.*, Series I, Vol. LIII, 425.

9 *O. R.*, Series I, Vol. III, 112.

10 Woodruff, *With the Light Guns*, 44.
     Lt. Omer P. Weaver was stationed at gun No. 1, Lt. William W. Reyburn at gun No. 3, and Lt. Lewis W. Brown at gun No. 4.

11 *Ibid.*, 44-45.
     All the casualties suffered by the Pulaski Battery occurred among the officers and men assigned to No. 1 gun. In addition, a shell from one of the Union guns splintered the caisson assigned to Weaver's piece.

12 *O. R.*, Series I, Vol. III, 66.
     The first firing that Sturgis heard was when Sigel's guns opened fire on the Confederate encampment. Sigel put his guns into action two other times. Apparently, only the first of these two bombardments was audible to Sturgis.

13 *Ibid.*; Holcombe and Adams, *Battle of Wilson's Creek*, 33-34.

14 Snead, *The Fight for Missouri*, 275.

15 *O. R.*, Series I, Vol. III, 76.
     The 1st Missouri was massed on a small elevated plateau. Capt. Nelson Cole of Company E had been shot in the lower jaw and had to be sent to the rear. Before being evacuated, the captain, although unable to speak, by the use of gestures sought to encourage his men. Capt. Cary Gratz had observed a force of Confederates led by a mounted officer carrying a Union flag approached his unit. Drawing his revolver, Gratz fired and knocked the Rebel officer off his horse but, upon striking the ground, the Southerner immediately arose and rushed through his lines. Gratz fired a second shot which pitched the Confederate headlong out of sight. The foe now opened fire, and the captain fell, pierced by five shots.

16 *Ibid.*, 82-83; Burke, *Military History of Kansas Regiments*, 3.

17 *O. R.*, Series I, Vol. III, 74.

18 *Ibid.*, 66, 79-80; Holcombe and Adams, *Battle of Wilson's Creek*, 92; Burke, *Military History of Kansas Regiments*, 3; "Field of Battle of Oak Hill," August 10, 1861, *With the Light Guns*.

19 *O. R.*, Series I, Vol. III, 78.

[20] Ware, *The Lyon Campaign in Missouri,* 317-318.

[21] O. R., Series I, Vol. III, 66.

[22] *Ibid.,* 84. The 2d Kansas was probably stationed on the hill north of Cawthorn's abandoned encampment.

[23] Burke, *Military History of Kansas Regiments,* 3; Holcombe and Adams, *Battle of Wilson's Creek,* 96.

[24] O. R., Series I, Vol. III, 66; O. R., Series I, Vol. LIII, 423; Holcombe and Adams, *Battle of Wilson's Creek,* 33-34.

[25] O. R., Series I, Vol. III, 66, 72.

[26] *Ibid.,* 72, 111, 113; Snead, *The Fight for Missouri,* 277.

[27] Woodruff, *With the Light Guns,* 45-46.

[28] O. R., Series I, Vol. III, 80.

[29] *Ibid.,* 72, 78.

[30] *Ibid.,* 80, 113, 116.

[31] *Ibid.,* 111, 115.

[32] Snead, *The Fight for Missouri,* 278.

[33] O. R., Series I, Vol. III, 115, 117.
Hyams' wing of the 3d Louisiana included the following units: the Pelican Rifles, Iberville Greys, Morehouse Guards, Pelican Rangers No. 2, Winn Rifles, Morehouse Fencibles, Shreveport Rangers, Pelican Rangers No. 1, and a few men from the Monticello Rifles. When Colonel Hyams formed his battleline, the Pelican Rifles and Iberville Greys were on the right.

[34] *Ibid.,* 127-128; Snead, *The Fight for Missouri,* 280.

[35] Holcombe and Adams, *Battle of Wilson's Creek,* 42, 46-47.

[36] *Ibid.,* 47.

[37] *Ibid.,* 42; O. R., Series I, Vol. III, 87.

[38] *Ibid.,* 117; Sigel, "The Flanking Column at Wilson's Creek," 305.

[39] Pearce, "Arkansas Troops in the Battle of Wilson's Creek," 301.

[40] Holcombe and Adams, *Battle of Wilson's Creek,* 47; Sigel, "The Flanking Column at Wilson's Creek," 305; O. R., Series I, Vol. III, 120.

[41] Holcombe and Adams, *Battle of Wilson's Creek,* 42; O. R., Series I, Vol. III, 87.

42 Holcombe and Adams, *Battle of Wilson's Creek*, 42-43; *O. R.*, Series I, Vol. III, 87; Sigel, "The Flanking Column at Wilson's Creek," 305.

43 Snead, *The Fight for Missouri*, 281; *O. R.*, Series I, Vol. III, 128.

44 *O. R..*, Series I, Vol. LIII, 433.

45 *O. R..* Series I, Vol. III, 112.

46 *Ibid.*, 117.

47 *Ibid.*, 87, 115-116; Holcombe and Adams, *Battle of Wilson's Creek*, 43.

48 *O. R.*, Series I, Vol. III, 112-113.

49 *Ibid.*, 113.

50 *O. R.*, Series I, Vol. LIII, 433.

51 *O. R.*, Series I, Vol. III, 114, 116-117. Rosser's command apparently remained at Sharp's following the rout of Sigel's column.

52 Pearce, "Arkansas Troops in the Battle of Wilson's Creek," 301.

53 Holcombe and Adams, *Battle of Wilson's Creek*, 47; *O. R.*, Series I, Vol. LIII, 433.

54 Sigel, "The Flanking Column at Wilson's Creek," 305.

55 *O. R.*, Series I, Vol. LIII, 433.
   The rest of Colonel Brown's command dismounted and marched to Parsons' assistance.

56 Holcombe and Adams, *Battle of Wilson's Creek*, 48.

57 *Ibid.*, 44, 48; *O. R.*, Series I, Vol. III, 91.

58 *O. R.*, Series I, Vol. III, 91-92.
   The three men with Lieutenant Farrand were Sgt. John Bradburn of Company D, 1st U. S. Cavalry, and Cpl. Charles Lewis and Pvt. John Smith of Company C, 2d U. S. Dragoons.

59 *Ibid.*, 92; Holcombe and Adams, *Battle of Wilson's Creek*, 45.

60 Sigel, "The Flanking Column at Wilson's Creek," 305.

61 *O. R.*, Series I, Vol. III, 89-90.

62 Sigel, "The Flanking Column at Wilson's Creek," 305; *O. R.*, Series I, Vol. III, 90.

63 *Ibid.*

153

[64] Sigel, "The Flanking Column at Wilson's Creek," 305.

[65] O. R., Series I, Vol. LIII, 425.

[66] Ibid., 425, 453; Sigel, "The Flanking Column at Wilson's Creek," 305.

[67] Holcombe and Adams, Battle of Wilson's Creek, 44.

[68] Ibid., O. R., Series I, Vol. LIII, 425; Sigel, "The Flanking Column at Wilson's Creek," 305-306.

[69] Holcombe and Adams, Battle of Wilson's Creek, 44.

NOTES ON CHAPTER VI

[1] O. R., Series I, Vol. III, 66-67, 77.

[2] O. R., Series I, Vol. LIII, 435.

[3] Ibid., 431.
Captain Guibor, while making a reconnaissance to the left, had been cut off by a Union patrol. The captain had escaped from the Federals, but he was unable to rejoin his battery until the battle was over.

[4] Ibid., 431-432.

[5] Burke, Military History of Kansas Regiments, 14; O. R., Series I, Vol. III, 67.

[6] O. R., Series I, Vol. LIII, 435.

[7] Snead, The Fight For Missouri, 281; O. R., Series I, Vol. III, 110.

[8] Snead, The Fight for Missouri, 282; O. R., Series I, Vol. III, 118-119, 126.

[9] O. R., Series I, Vol. III, 118-119.

[10] Ibid., 111-112.

[11] Ibid., 114; O. R., Series I, Vol. LIII, 423.

[12] O. R., Series I, Vol. III, 67; Holcombe and Adams, Battle of Wilson's Creek, 35.

[13] O. R., Series I, Vol. III, 83; Burke, Military History of Kansas Regiments, 11.
Lt. Matthew Malone was in command of the portion of Capt. Peter McFarland's company which participated in the charge.

[14] Burke, Military History of Kansas Regiments, 12. There were two 5th Missouri Infantry Regiments — one Union, the other Confederate.

15 *O. R.*, Series I, Vol. III, 83; Burke, *Military History of Kansas Regiments*, 12-13.

16 *O. R.*, Series I, Vol. III, 67, 81. Col. John F. Bates of the 1st Iowa, being sick, had not accompanied his regiment when it took the field.

17 *Ibid.*

18 Ware, *The Lyon Campaign in Missouri*, 318-320.

19 *O. R.*, Series I, Vol. III, 81, 83.

20 *Ibid.*, 80.

21 *Ibid.*, 74. Captain Woodruff reported that the unkindest thing he ever heard of Captain Totten was a remark of Capt. C. C. Danley's. In 1861 or 1862, Danley had said, "Totten was always a bosom friend of the man he drank with last." Woodruff, *With the Light Guns*, 47.

22 *O. R.*, Series I, Vol. III, 77.

23 *Ibid.*, 61-62; Wherry, "Wilson's Creek, and the Death of Lyon," 293.

24 Holcombe and Adams, *Battle of Wilson's Creek*, 35-36. Captain Herron reported that on the day of the battle Lyon was wearing his old uniform, that of a captain in the regular army.

25 *Ibid.*, 36; Wherry, "Wilson's Creek, and the Death of Lyon," 293; *O. R.*, Series I, Vol. III, 62.

26 *O. R.*, Series I, Vol. III, 67; Holcombe and Adams, *Battle of Wilson's Creek*, 36.

27 Holcombe and Adams, *Battle of Wilson's Creek*, 36.

28 Wherry, "Wilson's Creek and the Death of Lyon," 295; Woodruff, *With the Light Guns*, 47.

29 Wherry, "Wilson's Creek and the Death of Lyon," 295; Burke, *Military History of Kansas Regiments*, 15.

30 Burke, *Military History of Kansas Regiments*, 15; Holcombe and Adams, *Battle of Wilson's Creek*, 36.

31 Holcombe and Adams, *Battle of Wilson's Creek*, 36-37; Wherry, "Wilson's Creek, and the Death of Lyon," 295; *O. R.*, Series I, Vol. III, 84.
    Lyon was the first Union general to be killed in action in the Civil War. The place where Lyon fell was afterwards called "Bloody Point." By the time of the 1883 "Reunion," a pile of stones marked the site of Lyon's death.

[32] Holcombe and Adams, *Battle of Wilson's Creek*, 97; Wherry, "Wilson's Creek, and the Death of Lyon," 295-296.

[33] O. R., Series I, Vol. III, 84; Burke, *Military History of Kansas Regiments*, 16. At this time, the 2d Kansas was short two companies. Company I was serving as mounted infantry; Company B had been deployed as skirmishers and sent to watch the area on Osterhaus' right.

[34] Burke, *Military History of Kansas Regiments*, 16.

[35] O. R., Series I, Vol. III, 85, 119.

[36] *Ibid.*, 74, 80-81.

[37] *Ibid.*, 74, 119.

[38] Ware, *The Lyon Campaign in Missouri*, 322-323.

[39] Snead, *The Fight for Missouri*, 282.

[40] O. R., Series I, Vol. III, 119.
Subsequently, Greer was ordered to concentrate his command on the hill west of the Sharp house. Here Greer was joined by Major Chilton and the remainder of the regiment.

NOTES ON CHAPTER VII

[1] O. R., Series I, Vol. III, 62-67; Wherry, "Wilson's Creek and the Death of Lyon," 296.

[2] O. R., Series I, Vol. III, 67-68.

[3] *Ibid.*, 68; Holcombe and Adams, *Battle of Wilson's Creek*, 38.

[4] *Ibid.*

[5] *Ibid.*
Not only the officers, but also the enlisted men, subscribed to the belief that if Sigel arrived the day would be saved. The soldiers of the 2d Kansas also sighted a flag which they thought was the "Stars and Stripes" on the hillside to their left. Satisfied that Sigel was coming, Colonel Blair formed and dressed his lines. Three cheers were then given for "the victory deemed already won." Captain Russell rushed from his place in the line to where Blair was sitting on his horse. The captain grimly announced, "I tell you, Colonel, it's Manassas again." The words were scarcely out of the captain's mouth before the "fiercest fire of the day opened upon our lines from beneath the 'dear old flag,' and the battle was renewed with greater firing than ever." Burke, *Military History of Kansas Regiments*, 17.

[6] O. R., Series 1, Vol. III, 68, 77.

[7] *Ibid.*, 84; Burke, *Military History of Kansas Regiments*, 16.

[8] O. R., Series I, Vol. III, 68, 74.

[9] *Ibid.*, 78.

[10] *Ibid.*, 83.

[11] Ware, *The Lyon Campaign in Missouri*, 324-325.

[12] O. R., Series I, Vol. III, 112.

[13] *Ibid.*, 114.

[14] O. R., Series I, Vol. LIII, 431-432.

[15] *Ibid.*, 432.
Following the withdrawal of the 2d Arkansas Mounted Rifles and Hébert's detachment. Price's battleline was deployed from right to left as follows: Foster's regiment of McBride's division, the remnants of Cawthorn's brigade, Clarkson's and Hurst's regiments of Weightman's brigade. Slack's division, Guibor's battery, Clark's division, the 1st Arkansas Mounted Rifles, Kelly's regiment of Parsons' division, and Wingo's regiment of McBride's division.

[16] Snead, *The Fight for Missouri*, 282-283.

[17] Pearce, "Arkansas Troops in the Battle of Wilson's Creek," 302; O. R., Series I, Vol. III, 121, 123.

[18] Pearce, "Arkansas Troops in the Battle of Wilson's Creek," 302; O. R., Series I, Vol. III, 121.

[19] *Ibid.*

[20] Snead, *The Fight for Missouri*, 283-284.

[21] O. R., Series I, Vol. III, 123.

[22] *Ibid.*

[23] *Ibid.*, 121; Pearce, "Arkansas Troops in the Battle of Wilson's Creek," 302.

[24] Snead, *The Fight for Missouri*, 285-286.

[25] O. R., Series I, Vol. III, 68, 120; O. R., Series I, Vol. LIII, 432.

[26] O. R., Series I, Vol. LIII, 432.

[27] O. R., Series I, Vol. III, 68.

[28] *Ibid.*, 78.

[29] *Ibid.*, 68; Holcombe and Adams, *Battle of Wilson's Creek*, 38-39.

[30] *O. R.*, Series I, Vol. III, 74.

[31] *Ibid.*, 84.

[32] *Ibid.*, 84-85.

[33] *Ibid.*, 80.

[34] *Ibid.*, 63, 69; Wherry, "Wilson's Creek, and the Death of Lyon," 297.

[35] *O. R.*, Series I, Vol. III, 80.

[36] Burke, *Military History of Kansas Regiments*, 16.

[37] *O. R.*, Series I, Vol. III, 85.

[38] *Ibid.*, 68, 79.

[39] *Ibid.*, 80.

[40] *Ibid.*, 68; Ware, *The Lyon Campaign in Missouri*, 325.
In some sources, the spring near where the army halted is spelled, "Rose." During the retreat, it was discovered that, in order to insure the evacuation of the wounded, the body of General Lyon had been taken from the wagon in which it had been placed and left at the field hospital. Lt. Charles W. Canfield, with his command (Company D, 1st U. S. Cavalry), was sent with a wagon to recover the general's body. The lieutenant's party started for the battlefield. Before reaching the area, they found that the Confederates were in possession of the field and were busy gathering up their dead and wounded. In doing so, the Southerners had removed Lyon's body. Wherry, "Wilson's Creek, and the Death of Lyon," 297.

[41] Burke, *Military History of Kansas Regiments*, 4.

[42] Holcombe and Adams, *Battle of Wilson's Creek*, 40; *O. R.*, Series I, Vol. III, 69.

[43] *O. R.*, Series I, Vol. III, 69; Wherry, "Wilson's Creek, and the Death of Lyon," 297.

[44] *O. R.*, Series I, Vol. III, 69; Sigel, "The Flanking Column at Wilson's Creek," 306.

[45] Holcombe and Adams, *Battle of Wilson's Creek*, 59.

[46] Snead, *The Fight for Missouri*, 289.

[47] *O. R.*, Series I, Vol. III, 114.

[48] Snead, *The Fight for Missouri*, 286.

[49] Pearce, "Arkansas Troops in the Battle of Wilson's Creek," 303.

[50] *Ibid.*; *O. R.*, Series I, Vol. III, 746.

[51] Holcombe and Adams, *Battle of Wilson's Creek*, 59

[52] Snead, *The Fight for Missouri*, 287.

[53] *O. R.*, Series I, Vol. III, 119.

[54] *Ibid.*, 100, 106.

OFF TO THE WAR.

Appendix

Regiments, Commanders, Strengths, and Casualties of Each Command at the Battle of Wilson's Creek
Union Army
Brig. Gen. Nathaniel Lyon Commanding

	No. in Unit	Killed	Wounded	Missing	Total Casualties
First Brigade—Maj. Samuel D. Sturgis					
Regular Battalion	300	19	52	9	80
Capt. Joseph B. Plummer					
2d Missouri Infantry Battalion	150	15	40		55
Maj. Peter J. Osterhaus					
Co. I, 2d Kansas Infantry)					
(Mounted))					
Capt. S. N. Wood)					
Co. D, 1st U.S. Cavalry)	350		4	3	7
Lt. Charles W. Canfield)					
Co. F, 2d U.S. Artillery (6 guns)	84	4	7		11
Capt. James Totten					
	884	38	103	12	153
					(17.3 percent)
Third Brigade—Lt. Col. George L. Andrews					
1st Missouri Infantry	775	76	208	11	295
Lt. Col. George L. Andrews					
Regular Battalion	275	15	44	2	61
Capt. Frederick Steele					
Du Bois' Battery (4 guns)	66		2	1	3
Lt. John V. Du Bois					
	1,116	91	254	14	359
					(32.7 percent)

Fourth Brigade—Col. George W. Deitzler

	No. in Unit	Killed	Wounded	Miss-ing	Total Casu-al-ties
1st Kansas Infantry	800	77	187	20	284
Col. George Deitzler					
2d Kansas Infantry	600	5	59	6	70
Col. Robert B. Mitchell					
1st Iowa Infantry	800	12	138	4	154
Col. John F. Bates					
	2,200	94	384	30	508
					(23 percent)

Second Brigade—Col. Franz Sigel

	No. in Unit	Killed	Wounded	Miss-ing	Total Casu-al-ties
3d Missouri Infantry)					
Lt. Col. Anselm Albert)					
5th Missouri Infantry)	990	35	132	126	293
Col. Charles E. Salomon)					
Co. I, 1st U.S. Cavalry	65			4	4
Capt. Eugene A. Carr					
Co. C, 2d U.S. Dragoons	60				
Lt. Charles E. Farrand					
Backoff's Missouri Artillery	85				
Lts. G. A. Schaefer and					
Edward Schuetzenbach					
	1,200	35	132	130	297
					(25 percent)
Total	5,400	258	873	186	1,317

Average casualties for Union Army was 24.5 percent

Southern Army
Brig. Gen. Ben McCulloch Commanding

	No in Unit	Killed	Wounded	Total Casu-al-ties
McCulloch's Brigade—Brig. Gen. Ben McCulloch				
3d Louisiana Infantry	700	9	48	57
Col. Louis Hébert				
Arkansas Infantry	220	3	6	9
Lt. Col. Dandridge McRae				
1st Arkansas Mounted Riflemen	600	42	155	197
Col. T. J. Churchill				
2d Arkansas Mounted Riflemen	400	10	44	54
Col. James McIntosh				
South Kansas-Texas Mounted Regiment	800	4	23	27
Col. Elkanah Greer				
	2,720	68	276	344
				(12.6 percent)

Pearce's Brigade—Brig. Gen. N. B. Pearce

1st Cavalry	350	5	22	27
Col. DeRosey Carroll				
Carroll's Co. Cavalry	40			
Capt. Charles A. Carroll				
3d Infantry	500	25	84	109
Col. John Gratiot				
4th Infantry	550			
Col. Jno. D. Walker				
5th Infantry	650	3	11	14
Col. Tom P. Dockery				
Woodruff's Battery (4 guns)	71	3		3
Capt. William E. Woodruff				
Reid's Battery (4 guns)	73		1	1
Capt. John G. Reid				
	2,234	36	118	154

Missouri State Guard—Maj. Gen. Sterling Price
Rains' Division—Brig. Gen. James S. Rains

	No in Unit	Killed	Wounded	Casualties
1st Brigade	1,316	40	120	160
Col. Richard H. Weightman				
2d Brigade	1,210	21	66	87
Col. James Cawthorn				
	2,526	61	186	247
				(9.7 percent)

Parsons' Division—Brig. Gen. Mosby M. Parsons

Kelly's Infantry	142	11	38	49
Col. Joseph M. Kelly				
Brown's Cavalry	320	3	2	5
Col. Ben Brown				
Guibor's Battery (4 guns)	61	3	11	14
Capt. Henry Guibor				
	523	17	51	68
				(13 percent)

Clark's Division—Brig. Gen. John B. Clark

Burbridge's Infantry	270	17	81	98
Col. J. Q. Burbridge				
Major's Cavalry	273	6	5	11
Lt. Col. J. P. Major				
	543	23	86	109
				(20 percent)

	No in Unit	Killed	Wounded	Total Casualties
Slack's Division—Brig. Gen. W. Y. Slack				
Hughes' Infantry)				
Col. John T. Hughes)				
Thornton's Infantry)....	650	36	106	142
Maj. J. C. Thornton)				
Rives' Cavalry	284	4	8	12
Col. B. A. Rives				
	934	40	114	154
				(16 percent)
McBride's Division—Brig. Gen. James H. McBride				
Wingo's Infantry)				
Col. Edmond T. Wingo)				
Foster's Infantry)....	605	32	114	146
Col. J. A. Foster)				
Campbell's Cavalry	40			
Capt. Campbell				
	645	32	114	146
				(22 percent)
Missouri State Guard Total	5,171	173	551	724
				(14 percent)
Totals for Southern Army	10,125	277	945	1,222

Average casualties for Southern Army was 12 percent.

Picture Credits

The author and the George Washington Carver Birthplace District Association are particularly indebted to the publishers of the following publications for allowing use of their photographs and other illustrations in this book:

Struggle for Missouri

Page x

Battles and Leaders of the Civil War, Volume II
Inside front cover, pages iv, x, xiii, 5, 6, 18, 30, 35, 53, 63, 72, 74, 138, and 160

Missouri Sketch Book
Pages xi, xii, 12, 89, 115, 122, and 137

Civil War Art
Pages 13, 100, and 120

Leslie's Illustrated Newspaper

Page 25

The Lyon Campaign

Page 48

Index

Snyder, Colonel, 59, 62
Sokalski, Lt. George O., 56, 127, 129, 130, 140
South Kansas-Texas Mounted Regiment (see also Greer, Col. Elkana), 29, 32, 70, 89, 96, 162
Springfield, Mo., 1, 2, 4, 8, 9, 10, 11, 12, 13, 14, 15, 19, 20, 21, 27, 28, 29, 33, 34, 37, 38, 41, 42, 43, 44, 45, 46, 51, 52, 54, 56, 93, 94, 95, 96, 98, 121, 131, 134, 136, 137, 139, 140, 141
Stanley, Capt. David S., 10, 25, 45
Staples, Capt. Thomas E., 92, 93, 95, 97, 149
Steele, Brigadier General, 22, 23, 143
Steele, Capt. Frederick, 15, 16, 17, 25, 81, 85, 106, 124, 129, 131, 135, 147, 161
Steele, John, 54
Steen, Gen. Alexander E., 22, 32, 36, 67
Stockton, Capt. Job, 42, 146
Stone, Capt. G. Harry, 45
Sturgis, Maj. Samuel D., 11, 14, 29, 41, 42, 51, 78, 102, 106, 114, 121, 122, 123, 124, 130, 131, 134, 135, 136, 139, 141, 142, 144, 147, 151, 161
Sweeny, Gen. Thomas W., 2, 9, 10, 11, 46, 47, 48, 50, 140, 141, 144
Switzler, Capt. Theodore, 57, 84
T
Telegraph road, 14, 15, 16, 17, 19, 21, 23, 24, 25, 29, 34, 36, 41, 44, 45, 55, 66, 67, 68, 69, 70, 71, 76, 86, 87, 91, 93, 95, 97, 103, 124, 145, 149
Terrell Creek, 15, 29, 33, 34, 65, 66, 68, 69, 70, 95, 97
Third Arkansas Infantry (see also Gratiot, Col. John R.), 22, 126, 127, 128, 163
Third Arkansas Infantry Battalion (see also McRae, Lt. Col. Dandridge), 36, 75, 76, 142, 144
Third Louisiana Infantry (see also Hébert, Col. Louis), 32, 34, 75, 76, 85, 86, 87, 92, 124, 146, 152, 162
Third Missouri Infantry (see also Albert, Lt. Col. Anselm), 28, 70, 71, 72, 78, 93, 95, 97, 137, 140, 141, 142, 162
Thomas, Lt. Emile, 92

Thornton, Col. John C. C., 63, 164
Tod, Corporal, 88
Totten, Capt. James, 15, 23, 26, 27, 56, 57, 58, 62, 63, 65, 66, 78, 79, 80, 81, 89, 100, 106, 107, 113, 116, 117, 124, 125, 129, 130, 134, 144, 155
Townsend, Lt. Col. Edward D., 4
Tunnard, Maj. William F., 86, 124
Tunnard, Sgt. William H., 90, 92
U
Union Home Guards (Taney County, Mo.), 141
Utter, Sgt. Joseph, 50
V
Vigilini, Capt. John P., 88, 90
W
Walker, Col. John D., 75, 163
Walker, Leroy P., 19, 21
Ware, Pvt. Eugene F., 49, 50, 51, 52, 53, 81, 109, 118, 124, 131
Weaver, Lt. Omer P., 77, 78, 151
Weightman, Col. Richard H., 22, 29, 36, 65, 66, 72, 73, 77, 107, 108, 114, 116, 125, 126, 134, 135, 136, 144, 149, 157, 163
Wherry, Lt. William, 114, 115, 116, 121, 124, 134
White river, 34
Wilson Creek, 1, 34, 36, 37, 38, 40, 42, 45, 49, 51, 52, 55, 57, 59, 60, 61, 62, 65, 66, 68, 69, 70, 71, 73, 75, 76, 81, 82, 84, 85, 86, 88, 91, 92, 97, 106, 122, 123, 126, 127, 128, 143, 149, 150
Windsor Guards, 97
Wingo, Col. Edmund T., 103, 113, 127, 157, 164
Winn Rifles, 152
Wire road, 104
Wood, Capt. Samuel N., 84, 161
Woods, Lt. H. P., 141
Woodruff, Capt. William E. (see also Pulaski Arkansas Battery), 26, 33, 34, 36, 59, 62, 75, 77, 78, 79, 81, 84, 128, 145, 155, 163
Wright, Capt. Clark (see also Home Guard Companies), 12, 13, 14, 57, 84, 141
Wyman, Col. John P., 140
Y
Yates, Capt. Theodore, 99, 123
Yokermill road, 49, 54